Knit It Your Way

D0517663

Knit It Your Way

CHANGE THE YARN TO SUIT *Your* STYLE

CYNTHIA YANOK WISE

Martingale
& COMPANY

BOTHELL, WASHINGTON

Credits

President . . . . Nancy J. Martin
CEO/Publisher . . . . Daniel J. Martin
Associate Publisher . . . . Jane Hamada
Editorial Director . . . . Mary V. Green
Technical Editor . . . . Ursula Reikes
Copy Editor . . . . Liz McGehee
Design and Production Manager . . . . Stan Green
Illustrator . . . . Robin Strobel
Photographer . . . . Brent Kane
Text Design . . . . Trina Stahl
Cover Design . . . . Stan Green

Knit It Your Way: Change the Yarn to Suit Your Style
© 2000 by Cynthia Yanok Wise

Martingale & Company
PO Box 118
Bothell, WA 98041-0118 USA
www.patchwork.com

Printed in Hong Kong
05 04 03 02 01 00   6 5 4 3 2 1

Martingale
& C O M P A N Y

No part of this product may be reproduced in any form, unless otherwise stated, in which case reproduction is limited to the use of the purchaser. The written instructions, photographs, designs, projects, and patterns are intended for the personal, noncommercial use of the retail purchaser and are under federal copyright laws; they are not to be reproduced by any electronic, mechanical, or other means, including informational storage or retrieval systems, for commercial use.

The information in this book is presented in good faith, but no warranty is given nor results guaranteed. Since Martingale & Company has no control over choice of materials or procedures, the company assumes no responsibility for the use of this information.

Mission Statement

We are dedicated to providing quality products and service by working together to inspire creativity and to enrich the lives we touch.

Library of Congress Cataloging-in-Publication Data

Wise, Cynthia Yanok
   Knit it your way : change the yarn to suit your style / Cynthia Yanok Wise.
      p.   cm.
   Includes bibliographical references.
   ISBN 1-56477-313-2
   1. Knitting—Patterns.   2. Sweaters.   3. Yarn.   I. Title.
TT825.W57 2000
746.43'20432—dc21
                                                          00-026005

Dedication

∽

To my mom, Ann Yanok, for teaching me and sharing with me the joys of knitting.

Acknowledgments

Sincerest thanks to:

Frederikka Payne, whom I met at a knitting conference in Hoboken, New Jersey. I thank her for always having confidence in my design work, for being my friend, colleague, knitting buddy, pattern distributor, yarn provider, and for inviting me to Quilt Market in Providence, Rhode Island, where I met Beth Kovich in the Martingale & Company booth. I thank Beth for introducing me to Mary Green, and I thank Mary for being interested in my knitwear designs. I appreciate her kindness and coaching as I entered into the new and exciting adventure of writing a knitting book.

Ray Wise, my husband of seventeen years and my best friend. He has been of the greatest support in both of my careers. I thank him for putting up with my yarn stash, for working shows with me, for his calming words of wisdom, and for refreshing my memory about the square root of two.

Nancy Sturm, the best knitter a designer could ever have. She swatches, she knits sweaters, she follows my diagrams with blind confidence. She has always been there for me, and without her quick, expert skills, this book would not have been a reality.

Colleen Baldwin, for her expertise in knitting, for always challenging me with new projects and techniques, and for helping to meet the deadline by knitting the sweaters she did for this book.

Ursula Reikes, my editor, for her patience and understanding, for her technical prowess, and for her flexibility with my crazy schedule.

My parents, Ann and Frank Yanok, for all the opportunities and love that they have given me throughout my life. I love you both dearly with all my heart.

Erik Blazynski, my Web master, for his excellent skills in the development of my Web site. His ability to present my work in a professional and artistic manner has made another one of my dreams come true.

Les Ouellette, for being my true friend when times got tough. His kindness, understanding, support, zest for life, and great meals kept me going.

Brent Kane, for his excellent photography skills, and for making the photo shoot a less scary experience than I had imagined.

Terry Martin and Stan Green, for their encouragement, attention to detail, and kind words. I thank all the folks at Martingale & Company for making this book a reality.

Verilee Herpich, my good friend and massage therapist, for our conversations about life and growth, and for easing my pain after too much knitting.

All the knitting teachers and designers that I have studied with, for helping me to develop my skills and my own sense of design.

The magazines and yarn companies that have published my patterns, thus starting me on the pathway to this book.

My chiropractic patients, for their support in this other career that I have, and for the joy and love that they bring to my life.

To you all, I give my love.

Contents

Introduction

WE'VE ALL SEEN a beautiful garment that we just loved, but knew that it wouldn't work for us—too heavy, too light, or too expensive. With a little creative substitution, you can make a garment work for your climate, style, or budget, yet maintain the appeal that first caught your eye. This book is for knitters who do not wish to "follow the crowd," but who would rather stay attuned to ways of making a pattern work better for their needs. It is for the knitter who says, upon completing a project, "I knitted it my way!"

What a big country we live in, yet what a small world. We need clothing nowadays for the business trip to San Diego, the weekend in northern Maine, the wedding in Texas, and the vacation overseas. This book explores the possibilities of using different yarns for the same projects to yield diversified results. For example, I've included a vest design using wool in one version and cotton and novelty yarn in another to give you a choice of warmth, fiber, and "dollar" factors. This versatility means that a knitter in Minnesota can use wool to make the same vest as a knitter in Texas who prefers cotton. Because the fibers interchange so well, the vests will feel comfortable in each climate, yet both knitters will have achieved the same design results.

In addition, I've presented scarves in three different yarns and two different lace patterns, yielding six scarf possibilities. I also explore the dressy and sporty yarn looks.

You will learn the art of substitution— when this can be done and what the criteria are for making decisions. I've included yarn weights and yardage information to teach this concept so you will be able to answer the question "When is a particular yarn appropriate for a particular garment/style/design?" You'll also find out my secrets to swatching and discover its importance.

You probably need garments that work in a variety of situations: casual, dressy, business, chilly weather, warm weather, and perhaps travel abroad. You will learn how to make your own yarn and design choices based on your needs. The patterns in this book lend themselves to flexibility by being versatile: vests in different weights for different climates, sweaters in different fibers for different budgets, business wear that can translate well into a New Year's Eve garment. You'll find something for everyone, in every situation. And you'll be able to customize the garment for the individual, not make a carbon copy of someone else's design. Variety, versatility, vive la différence!

The Yarns

WE ALL HAVE a stash of yarn. Come on, admit it. You know where you've hidden it. It's time to fetch one skein of each yarn you're hiding and see what it can really do for you. You knew you had to have it when you bought it, but didn't know what you were going to do with it. Now is the time for your adventure.

Weights and Yardage/ Metric Information

FIRST, LOOK AT the wrapper on the yarn. Find out how many yards or meters are in the skein and how many ounces or grams are in it. This is extremely important information, and it doesn't matter which set of measurement units you use (yards and ounces for US, or meters and grams for metric); just be consistent. Look at the second skein of yarn. Is it the same number of ounces/grams and yards/meters as the first? If so, or if it's close, these yarns may be interchangeable in a project. How will you know? By knitting swatches, swatches, and more swatches! One thing you have to remember is that swatches are our friends! These seemingly useless coasters for ice tea (or beer) will give you more information than any teacher, designer, book, or other self-professed expert can ever hope to give. So get all your needles out and start swatching!

Let's start by looking at a cotton, a silk, and a wool yarn. I have chosen Garnstudio Paris, Silke, and Alaska. The information on the yarn wrappers is as follows:

Paris: 50 grams/approximately 82 yards
Silke: 50 grams/approximately 93 yards
Alaska: 50 grams/approximately 82 yards

Okay, so these three yarns are all in the ballpark as far as yardage is concerned. But how do you know if they all will give the same effect? Swatch them! That's how I found out. Not by magic, but by sitting on my porch night after night knitting swatches. I saw that if I did cables in Silke, they also looked great in Alaska. Sometimes I had to change the needle size to get the same effect. "Oh boy!" now you say, "I can't just use the same needles?" Maybe yes, maybe no. Is cooking an absolute? Is anything? How do you explain to someone exactly how much "a pinch" of cinnamon is? So size 7 needles for your taste may be size 8 needles for another. What flavor you want in your cooking is analogous to the texture you want in your knitting. Neither angel food cake nor lacy vests should be too heavy.

Now that I'm hungry, I'll explain what we are looking to accomplish.

The Art of Substitution

Choosing Yarns

WHEN I'M looking for yarns to substitute, I try to find yarns that are similar to the original project concept in weight, thickness, yardage, and texture. There are many variables to explore here. A wool may act similarly to a cotton if you know how to manipulate it properly. This means playing around with various needle sizes and knitting swatches! There's that *S* word again. Have you taken it to heart yet?

My Swatching Process

FOR SUBSTITUTING yarns, it is imperative to knit swatches with several different yarns and on several different needle sizes. To get started, I choose three needle sizes that I consider to be in the working range. Then I cast on thirty stitches and knit three swatches, one in each needle size. Sometimes I do three swatches in a long strip with a row of garter stitch between each swatch. I do the same with each yarn I wish to consider.

When I find the fabric texture I like, I try to match the gauges. This requires a larger swatch, particularly if there are many pattern stitches involved. For instance, when I finally chose the yarns for Intertwining Cables, I knitted a swatch that was 8" by 10". For simpler stitch patterns, I make swatches between 4" and 6" square.

Blocking the swatches is extremely important. Sometimes this requires steaming on the wrong side of the fabric. Sometimes wet blocking and pinning are necessary. Sometimes both processes are needed. Consider how the garment is going to be cleaned. If it will be hand washed and laid flat to dry, then this is how the swatch should be blocked. If dry cleaning is the method of choice, then steaming the swatch will give the proper results. I like to hand wash my garments, but I steam them before wearing, so I often wet block *and* steam my swatches!

After blocking, I measure for gauge by dividing the total number of stitches and rows by the exact measurements. If the gauges are close but not exact, I may re-block the swatches. Knitted fabrics are easy to manipulate, and as long as the result is what you want, it is definitely okay to block again to try to achieve the desired effect. If the results are not favorable, then I go back to the drawing board, so to speak, and try different needle sizes, and in some cases, different yarns.

When testing whether two different yarns can be substituted in a pattern, I start knitting the smallest piece of the garment first. If I am knitting a cardigan, I start with one front. I knit this up to the armhole, then knit the same piece with the other yarn. Now I can really tell if the two garments will be exactly the same upon completion.

It seems like a great deal of preparation, but if these steps are followed, there will never be disappointment after the garment is finished. Swatching should be fun and creative. Don't think of it as a chore, but as a wonderful opportunity for exploration!

With each project, you'll find a brief discussion about the choices I made for the project. And believe me, I was not always accurate in my choices at the first pass. (Swatch, swatch, swatch!)

Basics

Increasing

UNLESS OTHERWISE specified in the pattern, use the following "Make 1" (M1) increases.

RIGHT-SLANTING INCREASE

- On the knit side, insert the left needle from back to front into the horizontal bar between the last stitch worked and the next stitch on the left needle. Knit this strand through the front loop, twisting the stitch.

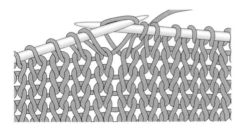

- On the purl side, insert the left needle from back to front into the horizontal bar and purl it through the front loop.

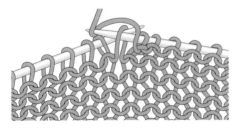

LEFT-SLANTING INCREASE

- On the knit side, insert the left needle from front to back into the horizontal bar and knit this strand through the back loop to twist it.

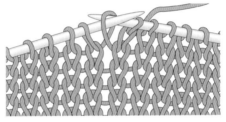

- On the purl side, insert the left needle from front to back into the horizontal bar and purl it through the back loop.

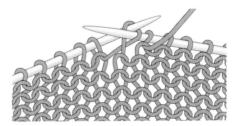

Decreasing

RIGHT-SLANTING DECREASE

- Knit or purl 2 stitches together.

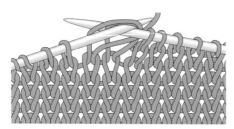

Knit Side

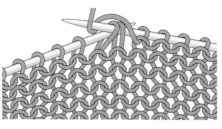

Purl Side

LEFT-SLANTING DECREASE

- Use SSK on the knit side of the piece. Slip 2 stitches knitwise, one at a time, from the left needle to the right needle. Insert the left needle into the fronts of these 2 slipped stitches and knit them together.

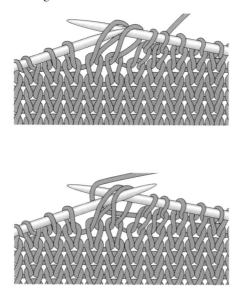

- Use SSP on the purl side of the piece. Slip 2 stitches knitwise, one at a time, from the left needle to the right needle. Return these 2 slipped stitches to the left needle as shown. Purl these 2 stitches together through the back loops.

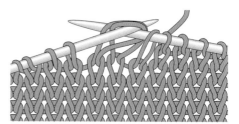

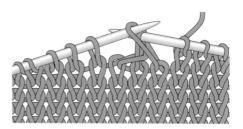

DOUBLE LEFT-SLANTING DECREASE

- On the knit side, slip the next stitch knitwise, then knit the next 2 stitches together. Pass the slipped stitch over the decreased stitch.

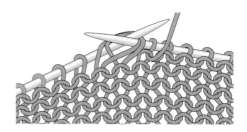

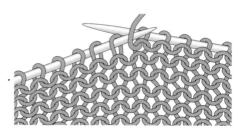

- On the purl side, purl 2 stitches together and return the stitch to the left needle. Pass the second stitch on the left needle over the decreased stitch and off the needle. Return the decreased stitch to the right needle.

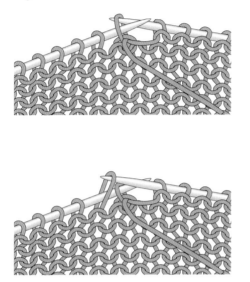

DOUBLE RIGHT-SLANTING DECREASE

- On the knit side, slip 1 stitch knitwise, knit the next stitch, pass the slipped stitch over the knit stitch. Return this stitch to the left needle. Pass the second stitch on the left needle over the decreased stitch and off the needle. Return the decreased stitch to the right needle.

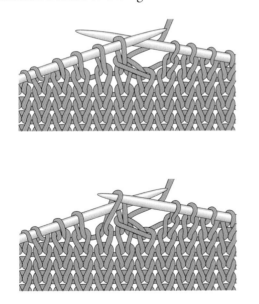

- On the purl side, slip 1 stitch purlwise, then purl 2 stitches together. Pass the slipped stitch over the decreased stitch.

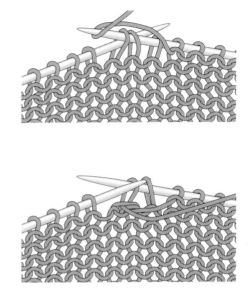

Joining Seams

MATTRESS STITCH

THIS invisible vertical seam is used to join side seams in stockinette stitch and is performed on the right side of the work. Insert the yarn needle under the horizontal bars of the first 2 stitches. Insert the needle under the corresponding 2 bars of the other piece. Continue alternating from side to side, inserting the yarn needle into the last stitch where the yarn exited.

Finishing Seams in Reverse Stockinette Stitch and Garter Stitch

This is performed on the right side of the work. Working into the stitches inside the edge, insert the yarn needle into the top loop on one side, then into the bottom loop of the corresponding stitch on the other side. Continue to alternate in this way.

Knot-to-Loop

This is an invisible seam on both sides of the work and is not bulky. It is performed on the right side of the work (with wrong sides together) unless otherwise specified. Insert the yarn needle into the knot of the stitch on one side, then into the corresponding loop on the other side. Go into the knot on the same side next to the loop you just came out of, then across to the corresponding loop on the other side. Continue in this manner across the work.

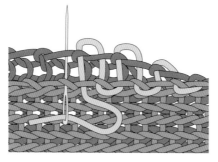

Three-Needle Bind Off (3-needle BO)

This is used to join shoulder seams. The seam is worked from the wrong side with the stitches still on the knitting needles. With the right sides of the pieces facing each other, insert a third needle knitwise into the first stitches on the 2 needles. Knit these 2 stitches together. Knit the next 2 stitches in this manner. Pass the first stitch over the second stitch. Continue in this manner until the last stitches are knitted. Pull the yarn end through the last stitch.

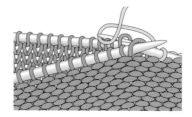

Crochet Bind Off

This can be used instead of the mattress stitch to join side seams and shoulder seams. With right sides facing, insert the crochet hook through both pieces, under the first full stitches. Catch the yarn and draw the yarn through. Repeat for the entire seam.

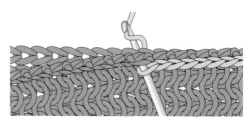

Kitchener Stitch

Hold the knitting needles parallel to each other. **Step 1:** Run the tapestry needle knitwise through the first stitch of the front needle and slip it off. Run the needle through the next stitch on the front needle purlwise and do not slip it off. **Step 2:** Run the needle through the first stitch on the back needle purlwise and slip it off, then run the needle through the next stitch on the back needle knitwise and leave it on. Repeat these steps until there is only 1 stitch left on each needle. Then, with the tapestry needle, slip the stitch off the front needle knitwise, and the stitch off the back needle purlwise. Bring the remaining yarn to the inside of the work and weave in the yarn end.

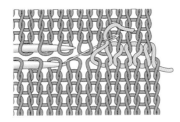

SEWING SHOULDER SEAMS TOGETHER

Perform as for the mattress stitch, but instead of bringing the needle under the 2 horizontal bars, bring the needle under each full bound-off stitch.

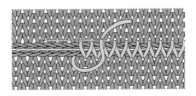

Sewing in Sleeves

To JOIN A vertical edge (sleeve) to a horizontal edge (back/front), insert the needle under a stitch inside the bound-off edge of the horizontal row. Then insert the needle under a bar between the first and second stitches of the vertical row. Continue weaving as often per inch on the vertical edge as there are stitches on the horizontal edge.

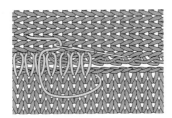

Picking Up Stitches

IN ORDER TO pick up stitches evenly, mark the work with pins every 2" and pick up the same number of stitches between each pair of markers. Insert the knitting needle under the entire edge stitch. Wrap the yarn around the needle knitwise and pull through the work.

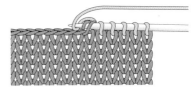

Adding Elastic to Ribbing

I USE A covered elastic that is available in many colors. Look for it in knitting stores and catalogs. On the wrong side of the work, thread the elastic through the back of each knit stitch and pull slightly to draw it in.

Crocheting

SINGLE CROCHET

BEGIN at the right-hand edge of the work. Insert the crochet hook into the fabric, catch the yarn and pull up a loop. Bring the yarn over the hook and pull it through the loop. *Insert the hook into the next stitch and draw through a second loop. Wrap the yarn over the hook and pull through both loops on the hook. Repeat from * to the end. Cut yarn and bring yarn tail through the last loop.

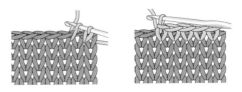

REVERSE CROCHET

BEGIN at the left edge of the work. Pull through a loop as in single crochet. Draw the yarn through the loop. *Go into the next stitch on the right. Wrap the yarn around the hook and pull it through the piece, then underneath the loop on the hook. Bring the yarn over the top of the crochet hook and draw the yarn through both loops. Repeat from * across work.

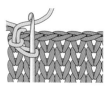 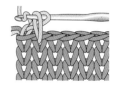

Blocking

ALL PIECES OF the garment should be blocked to the correct size and shape before assembly. This should be done on a blocking board. My blocking board consists of a 4-foot by 5-foot piece of plywood with a wool blanket and muslin fabric placed over it, wrapped over the edges, and stapled to the back of it. I use stainless steel T-pins and blocking wires. Blocking wires are wires that you weave into the edges of the knitted pieces before pinning the pieces onto a board with T-pins. (Look for them in knitting magazines and catalogs.) Using the measurements on the schematics of the pattern, lay out the garment pieces and pin. Depending on the blocking technique used for the swatch of the garment, either wet-block or steam the garment pieces and let dry or cool completely before removing from the board. Keep the schematic on file for future use, as when washing the sweater. This will ensure proper fit after cleaning.

Abbreviations

beg	beginning		pw	purlwise
BO	bind off		rep	repeat
CC	contrast color		rnd(s)	round(s)
ch	chain		RS	right side
circ	circular		RSR	right side row
CN	cable needle		sl	slip
CO	cast on		SSK	slip, slip, knit (see "Basics" for more information on decreases)
cont	continue			
dec	decrease		SSP	slip, slip, purl (see "Basics" for more information on decreases)
dpn	double-pointed needle			
EOR	every other row		st(s)	stitch(es)
inc	increase		St st	stockinette stitch
K	knit		tbl	through back loop
K2tog	knit two together		wyib	with yarn in back
kw	knitwise		wyif	with yarn in front
MC	main color		WS	wrong side
P	purl		WSR	wrong side row
P2tog	purl two together		yb	yarn back
patt	pattern		yf	yarn front
psso	pass slip stitch over		YO	yarn over

The Projects

BERMUDA TRIANGLE—*Safran*

Bermuda Triangle

SKILL LEVEL
Advanced Beginner

❧

SIZES
Small (Medium, Large, Extra Large)

❧

FINISHED MEASUREMENTS
Chest: 44" (48", 52", 56")
Length: 19" (21", 23", 24")

BERMUDA TRIANGLE—*Cotton Viscose*

YARN CHOICES

I WANTED TWO very different looks for this garment. First, I wanted something to wear over a black camisole for New Year's Eve. A slinky red Cotton Viscose turned out to be the perfect yarn. For the second variation, I wanted a top to wear to a summer barbecue or cocktail party, so I chose Safran, a vibrant variegated cotton, and added beaded fringe.

Cotton Viscose has 50 grams/120 yards, and Safran has 50 grams/174 yards. Since the yardage amounts are not exactly the same, I had to swatch. Cotton Viscose on size 6 needles yielded 4.75 sts and 6.5 rows per inch after steaming. Safran gave me the same gauge on size 5 needles after steaming. Because viscose stretches slightly, I was able to match my two swatches only after blocking with steam. I now felt safe that I would achieve the same end result. The lesson here? Be sure to block your swatches!

Materials

Version 1

- 6 (7, 8, 8) skeins of Garnstudio Cotton Viscose (54% Egyptian cotton/46% viscose, 50g/120yds)
- One pair of size 6 US (4mm) needles or *size to obtain correct gauge*

Version 2

- 4 (5, 5, 6) skeins of Garnstudio Safran (100% Egyptian cotton, 50g/174yds)
- One pair of size 5 US (3.75mm) needles or *size to obtain correct gauge*
- 102 (108, 116, 122) 5.5mm glass beads
- Steel crochet hook, size 13, or beading needle
- Crochet hook, size D

Both Versions

- Large stitch holder or spare knitting needle
- Stitch markers

Gauge

4.75 sts and 6.5 rows = 1" in pattern on size needles listed above

Take time to check gauge.

Pattern Stitch

Rows 1–4: Knit.
Row 5: Knit each st, winding yarn twice around needle.
Row 6: Knit each st, letting extra loop drop.
Rep rows 1–6.

Increase

MAKE increases by knitting into the front and back of the stitch. At the beg of the row, make inc in first stitch. At the end of the row, make inc in second-to-last stitch.

Double Decrease

THIS double decrease is made on the wrong side of the work: Sl 1 st kw, sl another st kw, return these 2 sts to the left-hand needle. Bring yarn to front. Sl the 2 sts pw (together) through the back loop. P1, pass the 2 slipped sts over. Bring yarn to back.

Single Decrease

AT beg of row, K1, then K2tog. At end of row, knit until there are 3 sts left on the needle; SSK, K1.

Directions

Back/Front

Making the Triangles

Make the back and front the same. CO 3 sts. Begin patt with row 1. On every even-numbered row, inc 1 st at each end as described above. Work until the sides of the triangle that are not on the needle measure 11" (12", 13", 14") (this is one-half the width of the back or front). End by working a WSR and by having an odd number of sts on the needle. Cut yarn and place this triangle on a stitch holder. Make a second triangle.

Joining the Triangles

Place both triangles on needle with RS facing you. Keeping in patt, work across first triangle, placing a marker before the last stitch. Make an inc in this last st. Knit the first stitch of the second triangle and place marker. Finish row. On the next and even-numbered rows, inc at each end as before, and make a double dec over the center stitch of the row as described above. On the odd-numbered rows, move the stitch markers out 1 st to prepare for the next dec row. When the height of the center line of double decreases measures 8" (9", 10", 10"), stop doing the inc on each end of row. Cont with the double dec in center; begin the single dec at each edge of EOR as described above until height at center line measures 15" (17", 19", 20"), ending with row 6 of patt. BO remaining sts.

Finishing

Join shoulders using mattress stitch. Measure down from shoulder seams 8" (9", 10", 10") or desired armhole depth. Sew side seams from bottom of garment to this point.

Beaded Fringe on Version 2

Cut yarn into 6" lengths. Thread 2 beads on each strand of yarn by using the steel crochet hook or beading needle. Knot both ends. Slide each bead to the knot. Trim excess yarn to ⅛". Fold yarn in half. With size D crochet hook, hang fringes 1¼" apart, starting at center front/back. Place 1 fringe on each side of both shoulder seams. Starting ¾" from center, place 6 fringes along each side of neckline.

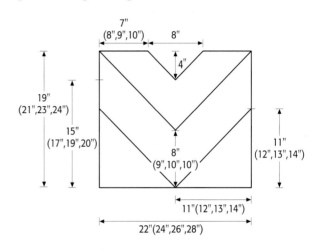

CABLE TWIST PULLOVER—*Morehouse Merino Wool*

Cable Twist Pullover

Skill Level

Advanced Beginner

⌘

Sizes

Small (Medium, Large)

⌘

Finished Measurements

Chest: 44" (46", 48")
Length: 24½" (25", 26")

CABLE TWIST PULLOVER—*Cotton Chenille*

YARN CHOICES

FINDING COMPATIBLE YARNS for this garment was challenging. I created this strange stitch in a loosely spun merino wool, which I loved. I didn't think that I would find anything that could compare to the original. Then I found the chartreuse Cotton Chenille. I had to make a slight concession on the pattern though. The baby cables in the ribbing didn't show up well in the chenille, so I altered the cable spacing by one stitch. That way, the chenille cables would make the same statement as the wool cables. Okay. No big deal. It took some swatching, but I got there.

Materials

Version 1

- 12 (13, 14) skeins of Garnstudio Cotton Chenille (100% cotton, 50g/76yds)
- One pair each of size 7 US (4.5mm) and size 8 US (5mm) needles, or *size to obtain correct gauge*
- One size 7 US (4.5mm) double-pointed needle (dpn)
- Size 7 (4.5mm) circular needle, 16" long

Version 2

- 8 (9, 10) skeins of Morehouse Farm Merino Wool (100% superfine merino wool, 3-strand weight, 2oz/145yds)
- One pair each of size 8 US (5mm) and size 10 US (6mm) needles, or *size to obtain correct gauge*
- One size 8 US (5mm) double-pointed needle (dpn)
- Size 8 (5mm) circular needle, 16" long

Both Versions

- Stitch markers

Gauge

3.5 sts and 5 rows = 1" in Twist Stitch on larger needles

Take time to check gauge.

Pattern Stitches

Cabled Ribbing for Version 1

Row 1 (WSR): *K1, P4; rep from *, end K1.

Row 2: Knit the knit sts and purl the purl sts as they face you.

Row 3: Rep row 2.

Row 4: *P1, sl next 2 sts to CN and hold to back. K2, K2 sts from CN, P1; rep from * to end.

Rep rows 1–4.

Cabled Ribbing for Version 2

Row 1 (WSR): *K2, P2; rep from * to end.

Row 2: Knit the knit sts and purl the purl sts as they face you.

Row 3: Rep row 2.

Row 4: *P2, TW2 (knit second st on needle, do not drop, knit first st, slip both sts off needle); rep from *, end K2.

Rep rows 1–4.

Twist Stitch

Row 1 (RSR): *K8, (K4, turn, P4, turn) twice. Place these 4 sts onto dpn. Rotate needle 360° to the right. Knit sts from dpn; rep from * to end.

Row 2, 4, 6, 8, 10, 12, 14, 16: Purl.

Row 3, 5, 7, 11, 13, 15: Knit.

Row 9: *K2 (K4, turn, P4, turn) twice. Place these sts onto dpn. Rotate needle 360° to the right. Knit sts from dpn. K8; rep from * to end.

Rep rows 1–16.

Directions

Back

With smaller needles, CO 66 (71, 71) sts for Version 1 or 68 (70, 72) sts for Version 2. Work in cabled ribbing for 3", inc 14 (11, 13) sts for Version 1 or 12 sts for Version 2 evenly across last WS row until you have 80 (82, 84) sts. Switch to larger needles. Work in St st for first 8 rows, then establish patt. **Center patt:** work 4 (5, 0) sts in St st, place marker, work in Twist patt, place marker, work 4 (5, 0) sts in St st. Cont until piece measures 24" (24½", 25½") from CO edge, ending with a WS row. **Shape neck:** work 26 (27, 28) sts, join second ball of yarn and BO center 28 sts, finish row. Working both sides at once with separate balls of yarn, BO 2 sts at each neck edge EOR once. Work until each side measures 24½" (25", 26"). Place each group of 24 (25, 26) shoulder sts on a stitch holder.

Front

Work as for back until piece measures 20½" (21", 22") from CO edge, ending with a WS row. **Shape neck:** work 34 (35, 36) sts, join second ball of yarn and BO center 12 sts, finish row. Working both sides at once with separate balls of yarn, BO 3 sts at each neck edge EOR twice, then dec 1 st at each neck edge EOR 4 times. Work until each side measures same as back. Place each group of 24 (25, 26) shoulder sts on a stitch holder.

Neckband

Join shoulders using 3-needle BO. With RS facing and circ needle (size 7 for Version 1 or size 8 for Version 2), pick up 80 sts along entire neck edge (omit the extra st in the chenille version). Work in cabled ribbing for 3". BO loosely in patt.

Sleeves

With smaller needles, CO 31 sts for Version 1 or 30 sts for Version 2. Work in cabled ribbing for 3", inc 5 sts for Version 1 or 6 sts for Version 2 evenly across last WS row. Switch to larger needles. **Establish patt:** work first 8 rows in St st, increasing as follows: inc 1 st at each end every 4th row 15 (10, 13) times, then 1 st every 6th row 1 (6, 5) times until you have 68 (68, 72) sts. *At the same time,* begin Twist patt on row 9. Work until piece measures 19" (19", 20") from CO edge or desired length. BO loosely in patt.

Finishing

Measure 9½" (9½", 10") from shoulder seams. Sew in sleeves. Sew side and sleeve seams.

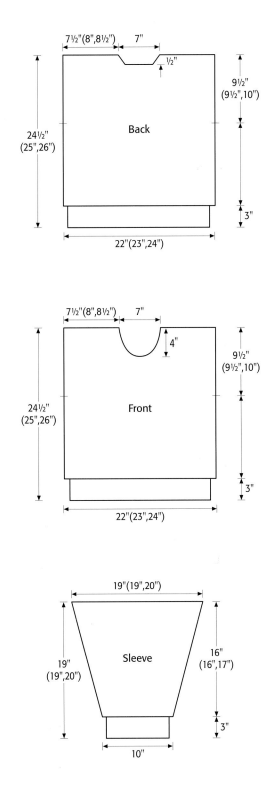

CAT'S EYES CARDIGAN—*Paris*

Cat's Eyes Cardigan

SKILL LEVEL
Advanced Beginner

❧

SIZES
Small (Medium, Large)

❧

FINISHED MEASUREMENTS
Chest: 44" (48", 52")
Length: 27"

CAT'S EYES CARDIGAN—*Alaska*

Yarn Choices

I HAVE TO admit that this was a relatively easy one to substitute. My tangerine Paris version was done on size 7 needles. I initially thought that I would have to go to size 10 needles in Alaska to get the same effect, since cotton is usually knitted on much smaller needles than wool. What a surprise when I found that my tension in Alaska on size 7 needles was equivalent to my Paris swatch on the same size needles!

But then again, look at the yardage. Each skein has 50 grams/82 yards. I should have guessed that even though Alaska is wool and Paris is cotton, they would knit up roughly the same. Lesson learned. Lots of coasters left over. I also swatched Silke for this cardigan and came out with the same gauge on size 7 needles, so there are three yarn choices for this one. Yee-hah!

MATERIALS

Version 1

- 17 (18, 20) skeins of Garnstudio Paris (100% cotton, 50g/82yds)
  OR 15 (16, 18) skeins of Garnstudio Silke (100% silk, 50g/93yds)

Version 2

- 17 (18, 20) skeins of Garnstudio Alaska (100% wool, 50g/82yds)

Both Versions

- One pair each of size 5 US (3.75mm) and size 7 US (4.5mm) needles, or *size to obtain correct gauge*
- Cable needle
- Stitch holders
- Small safety pins
- Six ¾"-diameter buttons

GAUGE

3.75 sts and 6 rows = 1" in Cat's Eyes pattern on larger needles
Take time to check gauge.

PATTERN STITCHES

Twisted Ribbing

On RSR: K1 tbl, P1.
On WSR: K1, P1 tbl

Cat's Eyes

Row 1 (RS): K4, *YO twice, K4; rep from * to end.
Row 2: P2, *P2tog, (P1, K1 tbl) into double YO, P2tog; rep from * to last 2 sts, P2.
Row 3: K2, YO, *K4, YO twice; rep from * to last 6 sts, K4, YO, K2.
Row 4: P3, *P2tog twice, (P1, K1 tbl) into double YO; rep from * to last 7 sts, P2tog twice, P3.
Rep rows 1–4.

Cable Panel

Rows 1, 3, 5, 7 (RSR): K2, P2, K4, P2, K2.
Rows 2, 4, 6 (WSR): P2, K2, P4, K2, P2.
Row 8 (WSR): P2, K2, C2B (sl 2 sts onto CN and hold behind work, P2, P2 from CN), K2, P2.
Rep rows 1–8.

DIRECTIONS

Back

With smaller needles, CO 96 (104, 112) sts. Work in Twisted Ribbing for 2", ending with a WSR. Switch to larger needles. **Foundation row (RS):** work 0 (4, 8) sts in St st, work Cable Panel over 12 sts, work Cat's Eyes panel over 24 sts, work Cable Panel over 12 sts twice, work Cat's Eyes panel over 24 sts, work Cable Panel over 12 sts, work 0 (4, 8) sts in St st. Cont with patt as established until piece measures 17½" from CO edge. Place a safety pin on each end to mark underarms. Cont until piece measures 26½". **Shape neck:** work 38 (42, 46) sts, join second ball of yarn and BO center 20 sts, finish row. Working both sides at once with separate balls of yarn, BO 2 sts at each neck edge EOR once. Work until each side measures 27". Place each group of 36 (40, 44) shoulder sts on a stitch holder.

Fronts

Make 1 and 1 reversed. With smaller needles, CO 48 (52, 56) sts. Work in Twisted Ribbing as for back. Switch to larger needles. **Foundation row (RS):** work 0 (4, 8) sts in St st, work Cable Panel over 12 sts, work Cat's Eyes panel over 24 sts, work Cable Panel over 12 sts, work 0 (4, 8) sts in St st. Work as established until piece measures 15" from CO edge. **Shape neck:** marking underarm as for back at 17½", dec 1 st at neck edge every 4th row once, then dec 1 st every 6th row 11 times. Work until piece measures same as back. Place each group of 36 (40, 44) shoulder sts on a stitch holder.

Sleeves

With smaller needles, CO 48 sts for all sizes. Work in Twisted Ribbing as for back. Switch to larger needles. **Foundation row (RS):** work Cable Panel over 12 sts, work Cat's Eyes panel over 24 sts, work Cable Panel over 12 sts. Inc 1 st every 8th row 10 times, then inc 1 st every 10th row once, keeping increased sts in St st at each edge. Work until piece measures 18" from CO edge or desired length. BO 70 sts in patt.

Back Neckband

Join shoulders using 3-needle BO. With smaller needles and RS facing, pick up 32 sts along back neck edge between the shoulder seams. Work in Twisted Ribbing for 6 rows. BO in patt.

Left Front Band (button band)

With smaller needles and RS facing, pick up 3 sts for every 4 rows along front edge of left front. Work in Twisted Ribbing for 6 rows. BO in patt.

Right Front Band (buttonhole band)

Pick up sts as for left front band. Work Twisted Ribbing for 2 rows. Beg 3rd row, make 6 buttonholes, evenly spaced: K2tog, YO. Work in patt for 3 more rows. BO in patt.

Finishing

Set in sleeves between safety pins. Sew side and sleeve seams. Sew back neck edges to front bands, using the knot-to-loop method (page 20) with WS facing you. Sew on buttons.

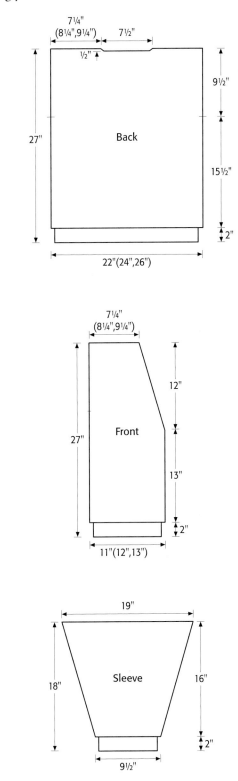

RIVIERA JACKET— *Ull-Bouclé and Silke-Tweed*

Riviera Jacket

SKILL LEVEL
Advanced Beginner

❧

SIZES
Small (Medium, Large)

❧

FINISHED MEASUREMENTS
Chest: 37" (42", 46")
Length: 22" (22", 23")

RIVIERA JACKET—*Bomull-Lin and Safran*

YARN CHOICES

THIS WAS A tough one. I wanted two extremes: a woolly version and a summery version. Ull-Bouclé on size 4 needles in seed stitch gave me a nice texture. To this, I added Silke-Tweed in a chevron pattern on size 5 needles. I was very happy with the result. But now what? What could I possibly use to make another jacket that would jazz me just as much as this one? Hmmm. . . I swatched Muskat. I swatched Tynn Chenille. Nice, but not the right gauge and too heavy . Then I tried Bomull-Lin. "Ooh, aah!" I thought! Great texture, right gauge on size 5s! But what would I use for the sleeves? Silke-Tweed is a very fine yarn at 50g/218yds, so I tried the Safran (50g/174yds). Since the Silke-Tweed contained wool, it filled out a bit more than the cotton Safran, and the result was fabulous! Well, okay, you decide.

Materials

Version 1

- 5 (6, 7) skeins of Garnstudio Ull-Bouclé (48% wool/32% acrylic/20% nylon, 50g/130yds) and 3 (4, 4) skeins of Garnstudio Silke-Tweed (52% silk/48% lamb's wool, 50g/218yds)
- One pair each of size 2 US (2.75mm), size 4 US (3.5mm), and size 5 US (3.75) needles, or *size to obtain correct gauge*

Version 2

- 7 (9, 9) skeins of Garnstudio Bomull-Lin (53% cotton/47% linen, 50g/93yds) and 5 (6, 7) skeins of Garnstudio Safran (100% Egyptian cotton, 50g/174yds)
- One pair each of size 2 US (2.75mm) and size 5 US (3.75) needles, or *size to obtain correct gauge*

Both Versions

- One set of size 2 US (2.75mm) double-pointed needles (dpn), or *size to obtain correct gauge*
- Stitch holders
- Yarn markers
- 3 buttons, approximately ½" diameter

Gauge

Version 1

4.5 sts and 8.5 rows = 1" in seed st in Ull-Bouclé on size 4 needles

6 sts and 8.5 rows = 1" in Brocade Chevron patt in Silke-Tweed on size 5 needles

Version 2

4.5 sts and 8.5 rows = 1" in seed st in Bomull-Lin on size 5 needles

6 sts and 8.5 rows = 1" in Brocade Chevron patt in Safran on size 5 needles

Take time to check gauge.

Pattern Stitches

Seed Stitch

Row 1: *K1, P1; rep from * to end.

Row 2: Purl the knit sts and knit the purl sts as they face you.

Rep rows 1 and 2.

Brocade Chevron (from *A Second Treasury of Knitting Patterns* by Barbara Walker)

Right Twist (RT): skip 1 st and knit the 2nd st, knit the skipped st, then sl both sts from needle together.

Left Twist (LT): skip 1 st and knit the 2nd st in back loop, knit the skipped st in front loop, then sl both sts from needle together.

Row 1 (WSR): Purl.

Row 2: K1, *RT, K8; rep from *, end RT, K1.

Row 3: P1, *sl 2, P 8; rep from *, end sl 2, P1.

Row 4: K2, *LT, K 6, RT; rep from *, end K2.

Row 5: K1, P1, *K1, sl 1, P6, sl 1, P1; rep from *, end K1, P1.

Row 6: P1, K1, *P1, LT, K4, RT, K1; rep from *, end P1, K1.

Row 7: (K1, P1) twice, *sl 1, P4, sl 1, (K1, P1) twice; rep from *.

Row 8: (P1, K1) twice, *LT, K2, RT, (P1, K1) twice; rep from *.

Row 9: K1, *(P1, K1) twice, sl 1, P2, sl 1, P1, K1; rep from *, end P1, K1, P1.

Row 10: P1, *(K1, P1) twice, LT, RT, K1, P1; rep from *, end K1, P1, K1.

Row 11: *(K1, P1) 3 times, sl 2, K1, P1; rep from *, end (K1, P1) twice.

Row 12: *(P1, K1) 3 times, RT, P1, K1; rep from *, end (P1, K1) twice.

Row 13: *K1, P1; rep from *.

Row 14: P 1, *RT, (K1, P1) 4 times; rep from *, end RT, K1.

Row 15: K1, *sl 2, (P1, K1) 4 times; rep from *, end sl 2, K1.

Row 16: K2, *LT, (P1, K1) 3 times, RT; rep from *, end K2.

Row 17: P3, *sl 1, (K1, P1) 3 times, sl 1, P2; rep from *, end P1.

Row 18: K3, *LT, (K1, P1) twice, RT, K2; rep from *, end K1.

Row 19: P4, *sl 1, (P1, K1) twice, sl 1, P4; rep from *.

Row 20: K4, *LT, P1, K1, RT, K4; rep from *.

Row 21: P5, *sl 1, K1, P1, sl 1, P6; rep from *, end last rep P5.

Row 22: K5, *LT, RT, K6; rep from *, end last rep K5.

Row 23: P6, *sl 2, P8; rep from *, end last rep P6.

Row 24: K6, *RT, K8; rep from *, end last rep K6.

Rep rows 1–24.

DIRECTIONS

Pocket Bands

Make 2. With size 2 dpn, CO 19 sts. Work back and forth in seed st for 11 rows. Purl 1 row. Use row 1 as RSR. Cut yarn, keep sts on dpn, and set aside.

Fronts

Make 1 and 1 reversed. With smallest needles and Silke-Tweed for Version 1 or Safran for Version 2, CO 43 (49, 53) sts. Work in seed st for 11 rows. Purl 1 row. Switch to Ull-Bouclé and size 4 needles for Version 1 or Bomull-Lin and size 5 needles for Version 2. Work 1 row (this is RS of work). Cont in seed st until piece measures 4" from CO edge, ending with a RSR. **Place pocket band:** with WS of front facing, work 12 (15, 17) sts, place WS of pocket band on RS of front, purl across pocket sts and center front sts (knit 1 st of each yarn together across needle). Cont in seed st to end of row. Work in seed st until piece measures 13½" (13½", 14½") from CO edge. **Shape armhole:** at side seam edge on EOR, BO 3 sts once, BO 2 sts once, then dec 1 st EOR twice until 36 (42, 46) sts remain. Cont in patt until piece measures 19" (19", 20") from CO edge. **Shape neck:** at neck edge on EOR, BO 5 (5, 6) sts once, BO 2 sts 3 times, dec 1 st EOR 3 times. *Work 2 rows , dec 1 st at neck edge at beg of next row; rep from * once. Work 2 rows or until piece measures 22" (22", 23") from CO edge. Place remaining 20 (26, 29) shoulder sts on a stitch holder.

Back

With smallest needles and Silke-Tweed for Version 1 or Safran for Version 2, CO 86 (98, 106) sts. Work band as for front. Change to Ull-Bouclé and size 4 needles, or Bomull-Lin and size 5 needles. Work in seed st as for front until piece measures same as front to armhole. Shape armholes as for front. Cont in patt until piece measures 21½" (21½", 22½"). **Shape neck:** work 22 (28, 31) sts, join second ball of yarn and BO center 28 (28, 30) sts, finish row. Working both sides at once with separate balls of yarn, BO 2 sts at each neck edge EOR once. Work until each side measures same as front. Place each group of 20 (26, 29) shoulder sts on a stitch holder.

Sleeves

With smallest needles and Silke-Tweed for Version 1 or Safran for Version 2, CO 50 sts for all sizes. Work in seed st for 11 rows, inc 4 sts evenly across last row (54 sts). Switch to size 5 needles (for both versions) and establish Brocade Chevron patt (row 1 is WSR). Place a marker at each end when beginning increases, and keep sts outside of Brocade Chevron patt in seed st. Working in patt, inc 1 st at each end every 4th row 15 times, then inc every 6th row 10 times until you have 104 sts. Work until piece measures 15½" from CO edge or desired length to underarm. Shape sleeve cap: dec 1 st at each edge *every row* 40 times. Work until sleeve cap measures 5". BO remaining 24 sts in patt.

Front Bands

With smallest needles and Silke-Tweed for Version 1 or Safran for Version 2 (RS facing), pick up 95 (95, 99) sts along front edge. Work in seed st for 11 rows. BO in patt.

Neckband

Join shoulders using 3-needle BO. With smallest needles and starting at edges of front bands, pick up 104 (104, 108) sts as for front bands. Work in seed st for 5 rows. **On row 6, make buttonhole:** work 3 sts, K2tog, YO twice, SSK, finish row. **On row 7, work the YOs as follows:** knit tbl in first YO, purl tbl in 2nd YO. Work in seed st for 4 more rows. BO in patt.

Finishing

Set in sleeves. Sew side and sleeve seams. Sew 1 button on neckband and 1 button in the center of each pocket band.

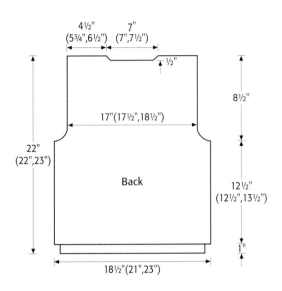

4½"
(5¾",6½")

7"
(7",7½")

½"

8½"

17"(17½",18½")

22"
(22",23")

Back

12½"
(12½",13½")

1"

18½"(21",23")

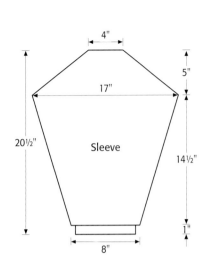

4"

5"

17"

20½"

Sleeve

14½"

1"

8"

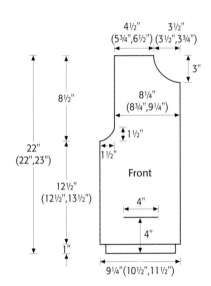

4½"
(5¾",6½")

3½"
(3½",3¾")

3"

8½"

8¼"
(8¾",9¼")

1½"

1½"

22"
(22",23")

Front

12½"
(12½",13½")

4"

4"

1"

9¼"(10½",11½")

KARISMA VEST—*Silke*

Karisma Vest

SKILL LEVEL
Advanced Beginner

❧

SIZES
Small (Medium, Large)

❧

FINISHED MEASUREMENTS
Chest: 34" (40", 46")
Length: 19" (21", 22")

KARISMA VEST—*Ull-Tweed*

YARN CHOICES

THIS WAS THE garment that started the concept for this book. In Connecticut, the weather changes so frequently that it made complete sense to me to make this vest for myself in two different fibers. I chose Karisma Ull-Tweed for the chilly weather and Silke for the nicer weather. Even though there is a difference in the amount of yardage in these two yarns (Ull-Tweed, 50g/120yds; Silke, 50g/93yds), the individual properties of the yarns surprisingly yielded the same gauge on the same size needles. Cool! It never hurts to swatch.

MATERIALS

Version 1

- 5 (6, 7) skeins of Garnstudio Karisma Ull-Tweed (100% pure new wool, 50g/120yds)

Version 2

- 7 (9, 10) skeins of Garnstudio Silke-Tweed (100% silk, 50g/93yds)

Both Versions

- One pair of size 7 US (4.5mm) needles or *size to obtain correct gauge*
- Crochet hook, size D
- Stitch holders
- Stitch markers
- 4 buttons, approximately ½" diameter

GAUGE

5 sts and 7 rows = 1" in pattern stitch on size 7 needles

Take time to check gauge.

NOTE: Steam swatch before measuring.

PATTERN STITCH

Multiple of 16 sts plus 2; see chart. Sts in parentheses are for medium and large sizes

Row 1: Knit.

Row 2 and all even-numbered rows to row 26: Knit the knit sts and purl the purl sts as they face you.

Rows 3, 5, 9, and 11: P9 (1, 9), *P10, K6; rep from *, end P2, P9 (1, 9).

Rows 7, and 13: K9 (1, 9), *K10, C6B (place 3 sts on CN and hold to back of work, K3, K3 from CN); rep from *, end K2, K9 (1, 9).

Rows 15, 17, 21, and 23: P9 (1, 9), *P2, K6, P8; rep from *, end P2, P9 (1, 9).

Rows 19 and 25: K9 (1, 9), *K2, C6B, K8; rep from *, end K2, K9 (1, 9).

Rep rows 1–26.

DIRECTIONS

Back

CO 84 (100, 116) sts. **Row 1:** Knit. **Row 2:** Purl. **Row 3:** Establish foundation row, following chart: work 9 (1, 9) sts, place marker, work patt over 66 (98, 98) sts, place marker, work 9 (1, 9) sts. Work until piece measures 11" (12", 13") from CO edge. **Shape armhole:** at each armhole edge, BO EOR as follows: for **Small**, BO 3 sts twice, BO 2 sts once, dec 1 st twice until 64 sts remain; for **Medium**, BO 4 sts twice, 3 sts once, 2 sts once, dec 1 st twice until 70 sts remain; for **Large**, BO 5 sts twice, BO 3 sts twice, BO 2 sts once, dec 1 st twice until 76 sts remain. Cont in patt until piece measures 18½" (20½", 21½") from CO edge. **Shape neck:** work 17 (20, 23) sts, join second ball of yarn and BO center 30 sts, finish row. Working both sides at once with separate balls of yarn, BO 2 sts at each neck edge EOR once. Cont until each side measures 19" (21", 22") from CO edge. Place each group of 15 (18, 21) shoulder sts on a stitch holder.

Fronts

Make 1 and 1 reversed. CO 44 (52, 60) sts. **Row 1:** Knit. **Row 2:** Purl. **Row 3:** Establish foundation row, following chart: work 1 st, place marker, work patt over 34 (50, 50) sts, place marker, work 9 (1, 9) sts. Keep the 1 selvage st in St st at front edge, and follow chart for remaining sts as indicated. Work as for back to underarm. Shape underarm, and *at the same time*, begin neck dec as follows: dec 1 st at neck edge EOR 19 times. When piece measures same as back, place 15 (18, 21) shoulder sts on a stitch holder.

Finishing

Join shoulders using 3-needle BO. With crochet hook, crochet armhole edges as follows: join yarn at seam, work a single crochet in every other st/row around. Work 1 reverse crochet in each single crochet around. Fasten off. For body of garment, join yarn at right front edge. Work single crochet as for armhole.

Then work 1 row of reverse single crochet as for arm-hole, making 4 button loops on right front by chaining 5 sts, starting 2" from bottom edge and evenly spacing them up to V point. Cont around neck, left front, and back. Fasten off. Sew in remaining ends. Sew on buttons, aligning holes of button with inner edge of crochet trim.

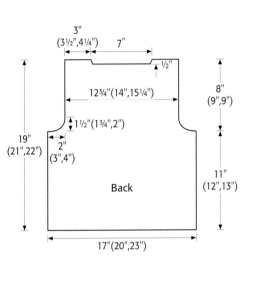

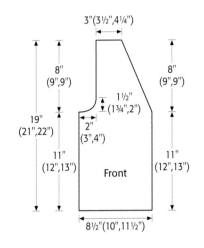

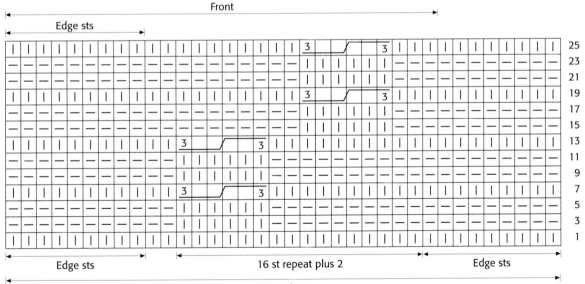

	K on RS, P on WS
—	P on RS, K on WS

 C6B (Place 3 sts on CN and hold behind work, K3, K3 sts from CN.)

On all even-numbered rows, knit the K sts and purl the P sts as they face you.

Chart repeat is rows 1–26.

LACE AND CABLE SOCKS—*Muskat (blue) and Angora-Tweed (gold)*

Lace and Cable Socks

Skill Level

Intermediate

෨

Sizes

Women's Small (Medium, Large)

Yarn Choices

HERE'S THE CHANCE for a summery pair of socks or a toasty pair of socks! The stitch pattern and yarns interchange very well, resulting in two very different effects. Wear with your best pair of sandals, or après-ski at the lodge!

MATERIALS

Both Versions

- 2 (3, 3) skeins of Garnstudio Muskat (100% mercerized Egyptian cotton, 50g/109yds) OR-2 (2, 3) skeins of Garnstudio Angora-Tweed (70% lamb's wool/30% angora, 50g/158yds)
- One set each of size 3 US (3.25 mm) and size 6 US (4.0 mm) double-pointed needles, or *size to obtain correct gauge*
- Stitch markers
- Elastic for ribbing (optional)

GAUGE

5 sts and 7 rows = 1" in St st on larger needles
Take time to check gauge.

PATTERN STITCHES

Twisted Ribbing

All rows: *K1 tbl, P1; rep from * around.

Cable and Lace

(multiple of 9 sts)

Rnd 1: *K3, P2, K2, P2; rep from * around.
Rnd 2: *SSK, YO, K1, P2, K2, P2; rep from * around.
Rnd 3: Rep rnd 1.
Rnd 4: *K1, YO, SSK, P2, TW2 (knit 2nd st on needle, do not drop, knit first st, slip both sts off needle), P2; rep from * around.
Rep rows 1–4

DIRECTIONS

The Sock

With smaller needles, CO 44 sts. Divide onto 3 needles. Work in Twisted Ribbing for 1½", inc 1 st in last st on last row. Switch to larger needles. Establish Cable and Lace patt. Work until piece measures 7" from beg, ending with rnd 4. **Divide for heel:** place 9 sts from needle #1 and 11 sts from needle #3 on one needle, leave remaining 25 sts on other two needles or place them on stitch holders. Cut yarn and join at beg of row. Work back and forth in St st on 20 sts, slipping the first st at the beg of each row. Work in St st for 20 rows. There will now be 10 slipped sts on each side of this section.

Heel Cap

Sl first st wyib, K13, SSK, turn. *Sl first st wyif, P8, P2tog, turn, sl first st wyib, K8, SSK, turn; rep from * until 10 sts remain.

Instep

Work across the 10 sts of the heel cap. Pick up and knit 1 st in each of the 10 slipped sts. Place marker. Work in patt across the 25 sts from the holders. Place marker. Pick up and knit in the 10 slipped sts as above. There are now 55 sts. Work around in St st except purl 1 st on either side of markers while working sts between markers in patt. As you work the following rnds, keep the number of sts between the markers constant (25 sts). K2tog, P1 in front of the first marker, and P1, SSK after the second marker every 3rd rnd 7 times (21 rnds). There are 41 sts remaining.

Foot

Work in patt and St st as established until the foot portion of the sock reaches the base of the little toe or 11 (15, 19) rnds, ending with rnd 4 of patt.

Toe Shaping

*K8, K2tog, knit to end.
*K4, K2tog; rep from * around, end K4.
Knit 4 rnds.
*K3, K2tog; rep from * around, end K2, K2tog.
Knit 3 rnds.
*K2, K2tog; rep from * around, end K3.
Knit 2 rnds.
K1, K2tog; rep from around.
Knit 1 rnd.
*K2tog; rep from * around.

Finishing

There are 7 sts remaining. Thread a sewing needle and sew end through remaining sts. Pull closed. Sew in all ends.

Twin Leaf Lace Scarf and Fir Cone Lace Scarf

SKILL LEVEL
Beginner

❧

SIZE
One size

❧

FINISHED MEASUREMENTS
Approximately 8½" x 60"

TWIN LEAF LACE SCARF—*Silke-Tweed and Camelia*

FIR CONE LACE SCARF—*Baby-Ull (teal) and Silke-Tweed (purple)*

YARN CHOICES

THIS IS PRETTY much a no-brainer. Don't you just love those? Three yarns—Camelia (50g/190yds), Silke-Tweed (50g/218yds), and Baby-Ull (50g/190yds)—pretty much equivalent. And after all, it's just a scarf! The two lace patterns I chose were almost equivalent in the total number of stitches they contained. So . . . this is not exact. Twin Leaf Lace Scarf has 54 stitches, and Fir Cone Lace Scarf has 59 stitches. Like I said, it's a scarf. No biggie.

MATERIALS

All Versions

- 3 skeins of Garnstudio Silke-Tweed (52% silk/48% lamb's wool, 50g/218yds)
  OR 3 skeins of Garnstudio Camelia (100% Superwash pure new lamb's wool, 50g/190yds)
  OR 3 skeins of Garnstudio Baby-Ull (100% Superwash merino wool, 50g/190yds)
- One pair each of size 3 US (3.25mm) and size 5 US (3.75mm) needles, or *size to obtain correct gauge*
- Stitch markers

GAUGE

7 sts and 6.5 rows = 1" in either lace pattern on larger needles

Take time to check gauge.

PATTERN STITCHES

Twin Leaf Lace (from *A Treasury of Knitting Patterns* by Barbara Walker)

(multiple of 23 sts)

Row 1 (RS): K8, K2tog, YO, K1, P1, K1, YO, SSK, K8.

Row 2: P7, P2tog tbl, P2, YO, K1, YO, P2, P2tog, P7.

Row 3: K6, K2tog, K1, YO, K2, P1, K2, YO, K1, SSK, K6.

Row 4: P5, P2tog tbl, P3, YO, P1, K1, P1, YO, P3, P2tog, P5.

Row 5: K4, K2tog, K2, YO, K3, P1, K3, YO, K2, SSK, K4.

Row 6: P3, P2tog tbl, P4, YO, P2, K1, P2, YO, P4, P2tog, P3.

Row 7: K2, K2tog, K3, YO, K4, P1, K4, YO, K3, SSK, K2.

Row 8: P1, P2tog tbl, P5, YO, P3, K1, P3, YO, P5, P2tog, P1.

Row 9: K2tog, K4, YO, K5, P1, K5, YO, K4, SSK.

Row 10: P11, K1, P11.

Row 11: K11, P1, K11.

Row 12: P11, K1, P11.

Rep rows 1–12.

Fir Cone Lace

(multiple of 10 sts plus 1)

Row 1 and all odd-numbered rows (WS): Purl.

Rows 2, 4, 6, and 8: K1, *YO, K3, sl 1, K2tog, psso, K3, YO, K1; rep from * to end.

Rows 10, 12, 14, and 16: K2tog, *K3, YO, K1, YO, K3, sl 1, K2tog, psso; rep from *, end K3, YO, K1, YO, K3, SSK.

Rep rows 1–16.

Seed Stitch

Row 1: K1, P1 across row.

Row 2: Purl the knit sts and knit the purl sts as they face you.

Rep rows 1 and 2.

DIRECTIONS

WITH smaller needles, CO 54 sts for Twin Leaf Lace Scarf or 59 sts for Fir Cone Lace Scarf. Work in seed st for ¾". Switch to larger needles. Work in seed st for 4 sts, place marker, work in patt across row, place marker, work in seed st for 4 sts. Work in patt as established until desired length, saving enough yarn for top border. Switch to smaller needles. Work in seed st for ¾". BO in patt.

Finishing

Block with steam through a pressing cloth on wrong side.

INCA JEWEL—*Alpaca*

Inca Jewel

Skill Level
Intermediate

❧

Sizes
Extra Small (Small, Medium)

❧

Finished Measurements
Chest: 36" (40", 42")
Length: 27"

INCA JEWEL—*Silke*

Yarn Choices

This may be my favorite sweater ever. I originally designed it in a worsted-weight alpaca. Then I found the Silke, and couldn't wait to knit this lighter-weight version. I love beads and cables together, but you may opt to eliminate the beads or the cables for a different look. Also, if you prefer a shorter version, the length of the stockinette stitch in the body will allow for a cropped style. Knit this in Alaska wool, Paris cotton, or Silke silk for the look and feel you want. What more could you ask for?

MATERIALS

Version 1

- 17 (19, 20) skeins of Garnstudio Paris (100% cotton, 50g/82yds)
  OR 17 (19, 20) skeins of Garnstudio Alaska (100% wool, 50g/82yds)
- One pair of size 8 US (5.0 mm) needles or *size to obtain correct gauge*

Version 2

- 15 (17, 18) skeins of Garnstudio Silke (100% silk, 50g/93yds)
- One pair of size 7 US (4.5mm) needles or *size to obtain correct gauge*

Both Versions

- 4 (5, 5) packages of 5.5mm glass beads, 140/pkg
- Small crochet hook to fit through bead hole, or beading needle
- Crochet hook, size E

GAUGE

4.25 sts and 6 rows = 1" in St st on size needles listed above

Take time to check gauge.

PATTERN STITCH

Cable 2 (C2): ⊠ Skip first stitch and knit second stitch on needle. Knit first stitch and slip both stitches off needle.

Bead 1 (B1): ◙ Pass small crochet hook through bead. Drop the stitch from the knitting needle, catch with hook. Draw stitch through the bead and replace on right-hand needle.

Half double crochet (hdc): Wrap the yarn over the hook and insert the hook into the work. Wrap the yarn over the hook, draw through the work only, and wrap the yarn again. Draw through all 3 loops on the hook.

Reverse crochet (rc): Single crochet from left to right instead of from right to left.

BEAD CABLE PATTERN

Multiple of 8 sts with 8-row repeat;
for bottom edges of front, back, and sleeves

Rows 1 and 5 (RS): *C2, K2; rep from * to end.

Rows 2, 4, 6, and 8: Purl.

Row 3: *K1, B1, K2, B1, K1, C2; rep from * to end.

Row 7: *B1, K1, C2, K1, B1, K2; rep from * to end.

Rep rows 1–8.

DIRECTIONS

Back

CO 76 (84, 88) sts and work 4 rows in St st. Work 22 rows of Bead Cable patt. Work even in St st. Inc 1 st at each edge when piece measures 8¾" and again at 17¼" until you have 80 (88, 92) sts. **Shape armholes:** when piece measures 17½", BO 2 sts at beg of next 6 rows until 68 (76, 80) sts remain. **Shape shoulders and neck:** when piece measures 26" from CO edge, BO 5 sts once at each shoulder edge, then BO 6 sts twice (7 sts 3 times; 7 sts once, 8 sts twice). *At the same time,* join second ball of yarn and BO center 30 sts. Working both sides at once with separate balls of yarn, BO 2 sts at each neck edge EOR once.

Front

Work the same as the back until piece measures 15¾" from CO edge. Work across 36 (40, 42) sts, and beg front Bead Cable chart on center 4 sts as follows: B1, K2, B1. Then every RS row, work 2 more sts each side of center sts in patt. *(Only RS rows are shown on chart.)* Purl all WS rows. *At the same time,* shape sides and armholes as for back. **Shape neck:** when piece measures 25" from CO edge, work in patt across 27 (31, 33) sts, join second ball of yarn and BO center 14 sts, finish row. Working both sides at once with separate balls of yarn, at each neck edge EOR, BO 4 sts once, 2 sts twice, then dec 1 st at each neck edge EOR twice. *At the same time,* when armhole is the same length as back, shape shoulders as for back.

Sleeves

CO 40 sts and work as for back through Bead Cable patt. *At the same time,* inc 1 st at each edge every 4th row 13 (11, 9) times and every 6th row 9 (11, 13) times until you have 84 sts. Work until piece measures 17" (17½", 18)" from CO edge. **Shape cap:** BO 2 sts at beg of next 6 rows. BO remaining 72 sts.

Finishing

Join shoulders using 3-needle BO. Set in sleeves. Sew side and sleeve seams. **Crochet border at edges of sleeves, bottom of garment, and neck edge:** Using size E crochet hook, join yarn and ch 2. Work a hdc in 3 of every 4 sts around. Join with sl st to top of ch 2. Do not turn work. Work 1 row of rc around. Fasten off.

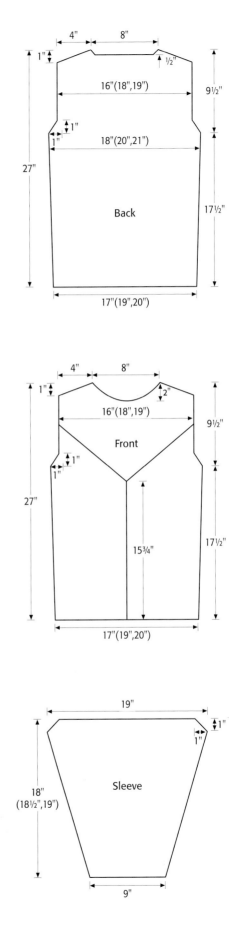

Front

← Medium

← Small

← Extra small

Border

8-st repeat

Repeat across

← Center front

Cont these 4 rows.

⬤ Bead 1 (see "Pattern Stitch")

☐ St st

✕ Cable 2 (see "Pattern Stitch")

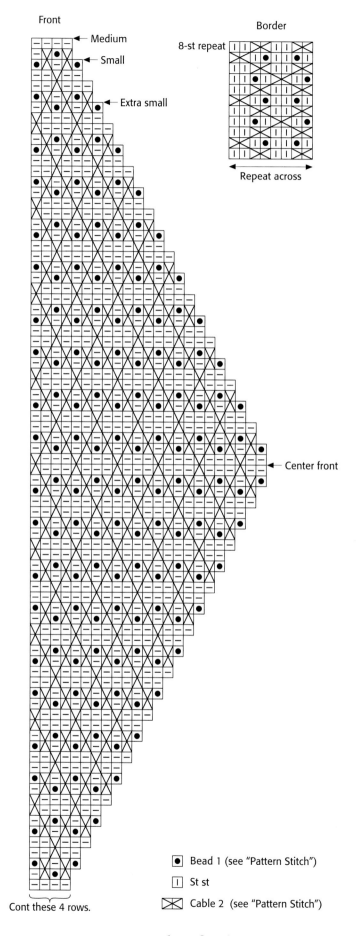

Baby Cable Socks

SKILL LEVEL
Intermediate

❧

SIZES
Women's Small (Medium, Large)

YARN CHOICES

FOR TWO VERY different looks and functions, I chose Baby-Ull and Silke-Tweed. The elasticity of the Baby-Ull makes for a more snug-fitting sock, and the Silke-Tweed gives a more dressy and elegant look. The yardage is close, and the gauges matched well, but the overall appearance of the Silke-Tweed sock is more relaxed. Camelia Superwash may also be substituted to make this pair of socks. The fit is still the same.

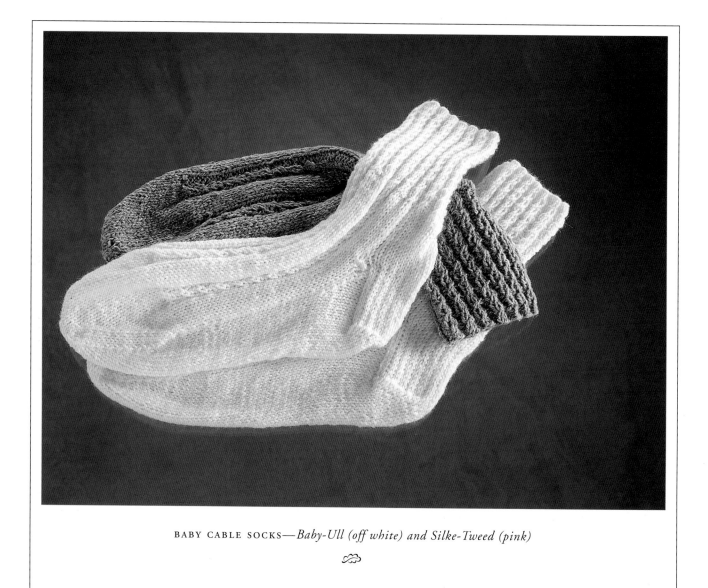

BABY CABLE SOCKS—*Baby-Ull (off white) and Silke-Tweed (pink)*

MATERIALS

Both Versions

- 2 skeins of Garnstudio Baby-Ull (100% Superwash merino wool, 50g/190yds) OR 2 skeins of Garnstudio Silke-Tweed (52% silk, 48% lamb's wool, 50g/218yds) OR 2 skeins of Garnstudio Camelia (100% Superwash pure new lamb's wool, 50g/190yds)
- One set each of size 1 US (2.25mm) and size 3 US (3.25mm) double-pointed needles (dpn) or size to obtain correct gauge

GAUGE

6.5 sts and 9 rnds = 1" in St st on larger needles
Take time to check gauge.

PATTERN STITCH

Baby Cable Ribbing

Rnds 1, 2, 3: *K2, P2; rep from * to end.
Rnd 4: *K2tog but leave on needle, insert right-hand needle between 2 sts just knitted together, and knit the first st again, then sl both sts from needle together, P2; rep from * to end.

DIRECTIONS

Cuffs

With size 1 dpn needles, CO 56 (60, 64) sts. Divide onto 3 needles; join, being careful not to twist sts, and work in Baby Cable Ribbing for 4", ending with rnd 4. Switch to size 3 dpn needles. Establish cable patt on instep as follows (this is rnd 1): K5 (6, 8), P2, K2, P2, K6, P2, K2, P2, K5 (6, 8). Cont rest of rnd in St st, purling first and last st. Cont cable patt on instep as established until piece measures 5½", ending with rnd 4.

Heel

Divide the sts so that there are 28 (30, 30) sts on first needle for heel and the remaining sts equally divided between 2nd and 3rd needles for instep; there are 14 (15, 17) sts on each instep needle. Work back and forth over the heel sts only. **First row (WSR):** *sl 1 st, P1; rep from * across. **2nd row (RSR):** sl 1 st, knit remaining sts. Rep last 2 rows alternately for 23 (25, 27) rows, ending with a purl row.

Heel Shaping

Row 1: Slip 1 st, K15 (16, 16) sts, K2tog, K1, turn. **Row 2:** Sl 1 st, P5, P2tog, P1, turn. **Row 3:** sl 1 st, K6, K2tog, K1, turn. **Row 4:** sl 1 st, P7, P2tog, P1, turn. Cont in this manner, always working 1 st more on each row until 16 (18, 18) sts remain. Work 1 row across the 16 (18, 18) sts. With first needle, pick up 12 (13, 16) sts along left side of heel. With 2nd needle, work in patt across all instep sts. With 3rd needle, pick up 12 (13, 16) sts along other side of heel, then with same needle, work across half of the heel sts. Keep the remaining 9 heel sts on the first needle; there are 20 (22, 25) sts on each heel needle. **Dec for instep:** On first rnd, work to last 3 sts on first needle, then K2tog, P1. Work in patt across 2nd needle. On 3rd needle, P1, SSK, work to end. On 2nd rnd, work across first needle, purling last st, work in patt across 2nd needle, P1, work across 3rd needle. Rep the last 2 rnds alternately until 56 (60, 60) sts remain. Work straight until piece measures 6" (6½", 7") from back of heel, ending with rnd 4. Discontinue ribbing patt and work in St st for ½" or until foot measures 2" less than desired total length.

Toe Shaping

Rnd 1: Knit to last 3 sts on first needle, then K2tog, K1. On 2nd needle, K1, SSK, knit across to last 3 sts, then K2tog, K1. On 3rd needle, K1, SSK, knit to end. **Rnd 2:** knit around. Rep these 2 rnds alternately until there are 20 sts remaining, ending with rnd 2. Place 10 instep sts on one needle and remaining 10 sts on second needle. Using kitchener stitch, weave sts together.

INTERTWINING CABLES—*Silke*

Intertwining Cables

SKILL LEVEL
Advanced Beginner

❧

SIZES
Small (Medium, Large, Extra Large)

❧

FINISHED MEASUREMENTS
Chest: 42" (44", 48", 52")
Length of short version: 21" (21, 22", 23")
Length of long version: 26" (26", 27", 28")

INTERTWINING CABLES—*Alaska*

Yarn Choices

Iᴏᴠᴇ ᴄᴀʙʟᴇꜱ and I love not having to do much finishing. This includes not having to knit borders. With a combination of knit and purl stitches stabilized by the cables, my dreams have come true! As I already learned from earlier projects, the Alaska and Silke yarns interchange well. But I still made large swatches and blocked them. The wool has much more elasticity than the silk, so I wet blocked and steamed my swatches to be sure of achieving the same gauge. I made the Alaska version full length and cropped the Silke version to show where the cable placement needs to be. The mock turtleneck is versatile for winter or summer. If cotton is the fiber of choice, Paris also works for this garment.

Materials

Short Version

- 13 (14, 15, 17) skeins of Garnstudio Silke, (100% silk, 50g/93yds)
  OR 15 (16, 17, 19) skeins of Garnstudio Alaska (100% wool, 50g/82yds)

Long Version

- 16 (17, 19) skeins of Garnstudio Silke
  OR 19 (19, 21, 23) skeins of Garnstudio Alaska

Both Versions

- One pair of size 7 US (4.5mm) needles or *size needed to obtain gauge*
- Size 5 (3.75mm) circular needle, 16" long
- Cable needle
- Stitch holders

GAUGE

5 sts and 6.5 rows = 1" in Intertwining Cable pattern on larger needles (Work entire chart as gauge swatch to accurately determine gauge.) *Take time to check gauge.*

PATTERN STITCHES

Intertwining Cable Pattern

See chart and key for body of sweater. On even-numbered rows, knit the knit sts and purl the purl sts as they face you.

Key for chart
☐ Knit.
⊟ Purl.
▱ Put 1 st on CN and hold to back of work, K3, P1 from CN.
▱ Put 3 sts on CN and hold in front of work, P1, K3 from CN.
▱ Put 3 sts on CN and hold to back of work, K3, K3 from CN.
▱ Put 3 sts on CN and hold in front of work, K3, K3 from CN.
▱ Put 4 sts on CN and hold to back of work, K4, K4 from CN.

Sleeve Cable

Put 4 sts on CN and hold to back of work, K4, K4 from CN.

Collar Cable

Rnds 1, 2, 3: K4, P4 around.
Rnd 4: *Place 2 sts on CN and hold to back of work, K2, K2 from CN, P4; rep from * around.
Rep rnds 1–4.

DIRECTIONS

Back

With size 7 needles, CO 108 (112, 122, 132) sts. Using row 1 of chart, knit the purl sts and purl the knit sts. **Next row:** Work 4 (6, 11, 16) sts in St st;

following chart, work Cable Panel over 19 sts; work Center Panel over 62 sts; work Cable Panel over 19 sts; work 4 (6, 11, 16) sts in St st. For short version, work until piece measures 12" (12", 13", 14") from CO edge. For long version, work until piece measures 17" (17", 18", 19") from CO edge. **Shape armhole for size Small:** BO 2 sts at the beg of next 6 rows, then dec 1 st at each edge EOR once. Leave 1 st at each selvage edge in St st. **Shape armhole for sizes Medium, Large, and Extra Large:** BO 2 sts at beg of next 8 rows until there are 94 (96, 106, 116) sts remaining. For short version, work until piece measures 20½" (20½", 21½", 22½"). For long version, work until piece measures 25½" (25½", 26½", 27½"). **Shape neck:** work 31 (32, 37, 42) sts, join second ball of yarn and BO center 32 sts, finish row. Working both sides at once with separate balls of yarn, BO 2 sts at each neck edge EOR once. Place each group of 19 (30, 35, 40) shoulder sts on a stitch holder.

Front

Knit as for back until piece measures 3½" less than total length of back. **Shape neck:** work 42 (43, 48, 53) sts, join second ball of yarn and BO center 10 sts, finish row. Working both sides at once with separate balls of yarn, at each neck edge on EOR, BO 4 sts once, BO 2 sts twice, dec 1 st 4 times. Work 2 rows, dec 1 st at each neck edge EOR once. Work until each side measures same as back. Place each group of 19 (30, 35, 40) shoulder sts on a stitch holder.

Neckband

Join shoulders using 3-needle BO. With RS facing and size 5 circ needle, pick up 56 sts along front neck between the 2 shoulder seams and 32 sts along back neck (88 sts total). Join and knit 1 rnd. Work Collar Cable patt, centering a cable over the center 6-stitch cable on sweater front. Work for 3½". BO in patt.

Sleeves

With size 7 needles, CO 52 sts for all sizes. Keep 1 st at each selvage edge in St st. Work 22 sts in reverse

St st, work center cable over 8 sts, work 22 sts in reverse St st. At each end, inc 1 st every 4 rows 7 times, then every 6 rows 13 times. Work until piece measures 17½" or desired length to underarm. **Shape sleeve cap:** dec 1 st at each end *every row* 8 times. BO remaining 76 sts in patt.

Finishing

Set in sleeves. Sew side and sleeve seams.

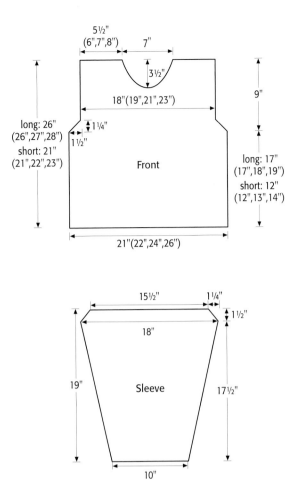

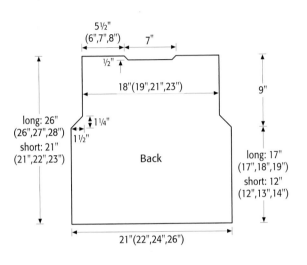

Repeat for extra left cable panel

Repeat for extra right cable panel

47
45
43
41
39
37
35
33
31
29
27
25
23
21
19
17
15
13
11
9
7
5
3
1

☐ Knit
─ Purl

Put 1 st on CN and hold to back of work, K3, P1 from CN.
Put 3 st on CN and hold in front of work, P1, K3 from CN.
Put 3 sts on CN and hold to back of work, K3, K3 from CN.
Put 3 sts on CN and hold in front of work, K3, K3 from CN.
Put 4 sts on CN and hold to back of work, K4, K4 from CN.

On even-numbered rows, K the K sts and P the P sts as they face you. Chart repeat is 48 rows.

DESPERADO—*Silke-Tweed*

Desperado

Skill Level
Intermediate

❧

Sizes
Extra Small (Small, Medium, Large)

❧

Finished Measurements
Chest: 34" (38", 42", 46")
Length: 19" (20", 21", 22")

DESPERADO—*Baby-Ull*

YARN CHOICES

THIS PAIR OF garments was a bit challenging. It was necessary to find lightweight yarns that would have a similar gauge in stockinette stitch and in the pattern stitch. I had to try various yarns, needle sizes, and pattern stitches before deciding on Baby-Ull and Silke-Tweed. Because the pattern should have an open look, the pattern-stitch swatches required some serious steaming.

When I began the design process for Desperado, I thought that I would add a ribbed trim or garter stitch trim to the edges and neckline. However, after all the finishing work, I steamed the pieces and saw that the edges were lying quite flat. I hate having to add anything to a garment that makes extra work for me so I let the steamed edges "be." I made a note in the pattern that as an option, two rows of garter stitch can be added to the front and back panel sections so less steaming is necessary. This is especially important if you substitute an acrylic yarn, as steaming would not be appropriate in this circumstance.

Materials

Version 1

- 3 (4, 4, 5) skeins of MC and 2 (3, 3, 3) skeins of CC in Garnstudio Silke-Tweed (52% silk/48% lamb's wool, 50g/218yds)
- One pair of size 3 US (3.25mm) needles or *size to obtain correct gauge*

Version 2

- 4 (5, 6, 6) skeins of Garnstudio Baby-Ull (100% Superwash merino wool, 50g/190yds)
- One pair of size 5 US (3.75mm) needles or *size to obtain correct gauge*

Both Versions

- Stitch holders

Gauge

5.75 sts and 8.25 rows = 1" in St st on size 5 needles in Baby-Ull and on size 3 in Silke-Tweed

6.5 sts and 5.25 rows = 1" in pattern on size 5 needles in Baby-Ull and on size 3 in Silke-Tweed

Take time to check gauge.

Pattern Stitch

Multiple of 2

Row 1: *Knit 2nd st, passing yarn twice around needle, knit first st in normal way, letting both sts drop from left-hand needle; rep from * across.

Row 2: P 1, *Purl 2nd st, passing yarn twice around needle, purl first st in normal way, letting both sts drop off left-hand needle; rep from * across, end with P1.

Rep rows 1 and 2.

Notes

- For Version 1 in pattern section, beginning with MC, work 2 rows of MC, then 2 rows of CC alternately.
- Optional: Knit 2 rows of garter st at the beginning of each front and back section to make the pieces lie flat without having to block them heavily.

Directions

Back

Side panels: Make 1 and 1 reversed. CO 34 (40, 46, 53) sts. Work in St st until piece measures 10" (11", 12", 13"), ending with WSR. **Shape armhole:** at armhole edge on EOR, work dbl dec (see pages 18 and 19) twice, then dec 1 st EOR 4 times until 26 (32, 38, 45) sts remain. Work until piece measures 13" (14", 15", 16"). Place each side panel on a stitch holder. **Center panel:** CO 42 sts. Work in patt until piece measures 13" (14", 15", 16"). Put the 3 panels on one needle with pattern panel in the center, making sure the left and right St st panels are appropriately placed; there are 94 (106, 118, 132) sts on needle. Work in patt until piece measures 18½" (19½", 20½", 21½"). **Shape neck:** work across 27 (33, 39, 46) sts, join second ball of yarn and BO center 40 sts, finish row. Working both sides at once with separate balls of yarn, BO 2 sts at each neck edge EOR twice. Place each group of 23 (29, 35, 42) shoulder sts on a stitch holder.

Front

Work as for back until pieces measure 13" (14", 15", 16"). Put the 3 panels on 1 needle. Work first side panel in patt, join second ball of yarn and BO center 42 sts, finish second side panel in patt. Working both side panels at once with separate balls of yarn, BO 2 sts at each neck edge once. Work until each side panel measures 1 row less than back. Dec 1 st at each neck edge on last row. Place each group of 23 (29, 35, 42) shoulder sts on a stitch holder.

Sleeves

Side panels: Make 1 and 1 reversed. CO 1 st. Working in St st, inc 1 st at seam edge EOR 11 times, then inc 1 st every 4th row 4 times. Work 2 rows; piece should measure 5". Dbl dec at seam edge EOR twice, then dec 1 st EOR 4 times. BO remaining 8 sts. **Center panel:** CO 86 sts. Work in patt until piece measures 6½". BO in patt.

Finishing

Block all pieces separately before assembling. Join shoulders using 3-needle BO. Using mattress stitch, join side and center panels of front, back, and sleeves. Set in sleeves. Sew side and sleeve seams.

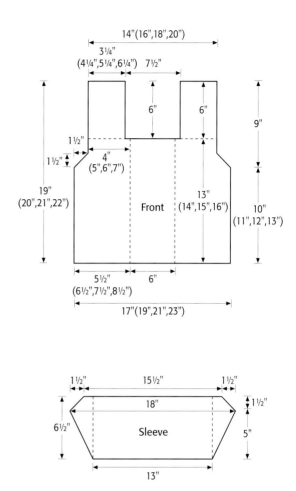

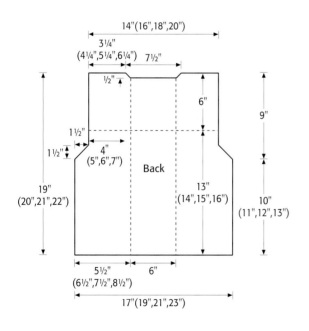

HOURGLASS STITCH JACKET—*Morehouse Merino Wool*

Hourglass Stitch Jacket

Skill Level
Intermediate

༺

Sizes
Medium (Large)

༺

Finished Measurements
Chest: 42" (46")
Length: 28"

YARN CHOICES

T HE HOURGLASS STITCH JACKET and the Hourglass Stitch Cardigan (page 95) have only the pattern stitch and needle size in common. Although this is an open stitch, the Morehouse merino jacket will provide warmth with its woolly properties, length, and doubled mock turtleneck—a rather classic and versatile look, typically New England to me. The Schaefer Yarn Company cardigan, on the other hand, is a more dressy and sophisticated look, with the fiber including a luscious, shiny silk. The hand-painted yarn that Cheryl Schaefer creates ensures that each sweater has a unique look.

MATERIALS

- 13 (15) skeins of Morehouse Farm Merino Wool (100% superfine merino wool, 3-strand weight, 2 oz/145 yds)
- One pair each of size 5 US (3.75mm) and size 7 US (4.5mm) needles, or *size to obtain correct gauge*
- One each of size 5 US (3.75mm) and size 7 US (4.5mm) circular needles, 36" long, or *size to obtain correct gauge*
- Stitch holders
- Stitch markers
- Twelve ¾"-diameter buttons

GAUGE

5 sts and 8 rows = 1" in Hourglass Eyelet stitch on larger needles

Take time to check gauge.

NOTE: This garment is made in one piece to the underarm, then divided into the back and two fronts. Sleeves are knitted separately and sewn in.

PATTERN STITCH

Hourglass Eyelet (from *A Treasury of Knitting Patterns* by Barbara Walker)

Multiple of 6 sts plus 1

Row 1 (RS): K6, *P1, K5; rep from *, end K1.

Row 2: K1, *P5, K1; rep from *.

Row 3: K1, *YO, SSK, P1, K2tog, YO, K1; rep from *.

Row 4: K1, P2, *K1, P5; rep from * to last 4 sts, end K1, P2, K1.

Row 5: K3, *P1, K5; rep from *, end last rep K3.

Row 6: Rep row 4.

Row 7: K1, *K2tog, YO, K1, YO, SSK, P1; rep from *, end last rep K1 instead of P1.

Row 8: Rep row 2.

Rep rows 1–8.

DIRECTIONS

Jacket Body

With smaller circ needles, CO 207 (225) sts. Work K1, P1 ribbing for 2". With larger circ needles, beg Hourglass Eyelet patt, keeping first and last st of row as selvage sts by knitting them in St st (knit on right side, purl on wrong side). Place marker after first st and before last st of row. Work in patt until piece measures 18" from CO edge. Divide for underarm (note patt row number). Each front has 52 (55) sts. Back has 103 (115) sts. Leave back and 1 front on circ needle.

Fronts

Cont on 1 front with straight needles for 8". **Shape neck:** at neck edge on EOR, BO 4 sts twice, 3 sts once, 2 sts once, 1 st once, 2 sts once. Dec 1 st at neck edge EOR twice. Work until piece measures 10" from armhole division. Place 34 (37) shoulder sts on a stitch holder. Work other front, reversing shaping.

Back

Work on center 103 (115) sts. Work until piece measures 9½" from underarm. **Divide for neck:** work 36 (39) sts, join second ball of yarn and BO center 31 (37) sts, finish row. Working both sides at once with separate balls of yarn, dec 1 st at each neck edge EOR twice. Work until each side measures 10" from underarm. Place each group of 34 (37) shoulder sts on a stitch holder.

Sleeves (same for both sizes)

With smaller needles, CO 57 sts. K1, P1 for 2". With larger needles, beg patt, keeping selvage sts in St st as for jacket body. Inc 1 st at each end every 4th row 11 times, then every 6th row 12 times. Work until piece measures 18" from CO edge. BO loosely in patt.

Button Band (right edge)

Join shoulders using 3-needle BO. With RS facing and smaller needles, pick up 139 sts evenly along left front edge. Work in K1, P1 ribbing for 8 rows. BO in patt.

Buttonhole Band (left edge)

Pick up sts as for button band. On 4th row, make buttonholes on the following sts (counting from bottom of jacket): sts 6 and 7, 20 and 21, 34 and 35, 48 and 49, 62 and 63, 76 and 77, 90 and 91, 104 and 105, 118 and 119, 132 and 133. **Buttonhole:** Sl 1 st as if to purl. Bring yarn to front and leave it there. Sl 1, pass first st over 2nd, put last st on left-hand needle, reversing it. Reverse last st on right-hand needle. Pull yarn tightly, lay it over right-hand needle from front to back and pass turned st over it. Make 2 firm backward loops over right-hand needle, K2tog, cont to next buttonhole.

Neckband

With RS facing and smaller needles, pick up 89 sts along neck edge and bands. Work in K1, P1 ribbing for 3 rows, beg and ending with P1. On 4th row, make buttonhole on 5th and 6th sts from neck edge (be sure this lines up with other buttonholes). On row 12, make another buttonhole. Work until 16 rows are completed. Make a turning row (purl sts across row if RS is facing, knit sts across row if WS is facing). Work in K1, P1 ribbing for 4 rows. Make buttonhole on next row. Work in K1, P1 ribbing for 7 rows. Make buttonhole on next row. Work in K1, P1 ribbing for 3 more rows. BO in patt.

Finishing

Fold neckband to inside of jacket and slip stitch in place. Set in sleeves. Sew side and sleeve seams. Finish buttonholes of neckband with buttonhole stitch. Sew on buttons.

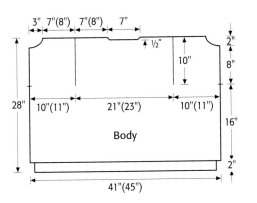

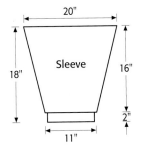

HOURGLASS STITCH CARDIGAN—*Schaefer Helene*

Hourglass Stitch Cardigan

SKILL LEVEL
Advanced Beginner

⋙

SIZES
Small (Medium)

⋙

FINISHED MEASUREMENTS
Chest: 43" (49")
Length: 24" (25")

MATERIALS

- Approximately 1500 (1750) yds of Helene, from Schaefer Yarn Company (50% wool/50% silk, 24 (28) oz each hank)
- One pair each of size 5 US (3.75mm) and size 7 US (4.5mm) needles, or *size to obtain correct gauge*
- Nine ¾"-diameter buttons

GAUGE

5 sts and 8 rows = 1" in Hourglass Eyelet stitch on larger needles

Take time to check gauge.

PATTERN STITCH

Hourglass Eyelet (from *A Treasury of Knitting Patterns* by Barbara Walker)

(multiple of 6 sts plus 1)

Row 1 (RS): K6, *P1, K5; rep from *, end K1.

Row 2: K1, *P5, K1; rep from *.

Row 3: K1, *YO, SSK, P1, K2tog, YO, K1; rep from *.

Row 4: K1, P2, *K1, P5; rep from * to last 4 sts, end K1, P2, K1.

Row 5: K3, *P1, K5; rep from *, end last rep K3.

Row 6: Rep row 4.

Row 7: K1, *K2tog, YO, K1, YO, SSK, P1; rep from *, end last rep K1 instead of P1.

Row 8: Rep row 2.

Rep rows 1–8.

DIRECTIONS

Back

With smaller needles, CO 92 (102) sts. Work in K 1, P 1 ribbing for 2", inc 17 (19) sts evenly across last WS row until you have 109 (121) sts. Switch to larger needles and beg patt, keeping first and last st of row as selvage sts by knitting them in St st (knit on right side, purl on wrong side). Work in patt until piece measures 23½" (24½") from CO edge. Work 37 (40) sts, join second ball of yarn and BO center 35 (41) sts, finish row. Working both sides at once with separate balls of yarn, BO 2 sts at each neck edge EOR once. Place each group of 35 (38) shoulder sts on a stitch holder.

Fronts

Make 1 and 1 reversed. With smaller needles, CO 46 (52) sts. Work in K1, P1 ribbing for 2", inc 9 sts evenly across last WS row until you have 55 (61) sts. Switch to larger needles. Work in patt, keeping first and last st of row as selvage as for back, until piece measures 22" (23") from CO edge. **Shape neck:** *For size **Small,** at neck edge on EOR BO 7 sts once, BO 4 sts once, BO 2 sts 3 times, dec 1 st EOR 3 times until you have 35 sts remaining; for size **Medium,** on EOR BO 8 sts once, BO 4 sts once, BO 3 sts once, BO 2 sts 3 times, dec 1 st EOR 2 times until you have 38 sts remaining. Work until piece measures same as back. Place 35 (38) shoulder sts on a stitch holder.

Sleeves

With smaller needles, CO 46 (52) sts. Work in K1, P1 ribbing for 2", inc 9 sts evenly across last WS row until you have 55 (61) sts. Switch to larger needles and work in patt stitch, keeping first and last st of row as selvage as for back. Inc 1 st each end every 4 rows 7 (3) times then every 6 rows 16 (20) times, working new sts into patt until you have 101 (107) sts. Work until piece measures 18" (19") from CO edge or desired length. BO all sts in patt.

Neckband

Join shoulders using 3-needle BO. Pick up 84 (92) sts evenly along neck edge. With smaller needles, work in K1, P1 ribbing for 2". BO in patt.

Button Band

With smaller needles and RS facing, pick up 3 sts for every 4 rows evenly along left front edge and neckband. Work in K1, P1 ribbing for 1". BO in patt.

Buttonhole Band

Work as for button band for ½". Make 9 buttonholes approximately 2½" apart: K2tog, YO. Work in established ribbing until piece measures 1". BO in patt.

Finishing

Set in sleeves. Sew side and sleeve seams. Sew on buttons.

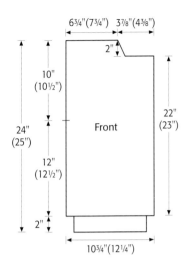

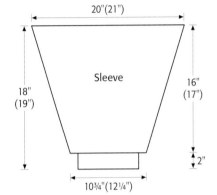

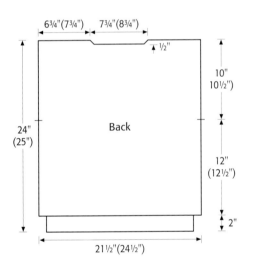

ANDEAN ARTISTRY—*Alpaca Fina*

Andean Artistry

Skill Level

Intermediate

❧

Sizes

Extra Small (Small, Medium, Large)

❧

Finished Measurements

Chest: 35" (38", 40", 42")
Length: 19½" (21", 21", 23")

ANDEAN ARTISTRY—*Silke-Tweed*

Yarn Choices

This is one of my favorite cardigans. After studying Andean art history books containing textiles, pottery, and other artwork, I created my own Fair Isle (jacquard) pattern by doodling on graph paper. I kept changing colors and came up with so many different combinations I liked that it was difficult to decide on only two versions for this project. I looked for fibers that would give me a South American look. I chose Alpaca Fina and Silke-Tweed. Because they are both 50g/218yds, I felt I would achieve similar results. The Alpaca Fina version gives a fluffier, softer look and feel, while the Silke-Tweed is more crisp. Either way, this is a very stylish open cardigan with many color possibilities.

MATERIALS

Version 1

- 10 skeins of black (MC) Alpaca Fina, 2 skeins *each* of green and rust, and 3 skeins of gold Alpaca Fina (50g/218yds)

Version 2

- 7(8,8,9) skeins of #13-rust (MC), 2 skeins *each* of #12-gold and #14-green, and 3 skeins of #06-black Garnstudio Silke-Tweed (52% silk/48% lamb's wool, 50g/218yds)

Both Versions

- One pair each of size 3 US (3.25mm) and size 4 US (3.5mm) needles, or *size to obtain correct gauge*
- Crochet hook, size E

GAUGE

Both Versions

6.5 sts and 9.5 rows = 1" in St st on size 4 needles

7.25 sts and 9 rows = 1" in Fair Isle pattern on size 4 needles

Take time to check gauge.

NOTES

- Steam gauge swatches before measuring.
- Borders: Use MC and gold for Version 1. Use MC and black for Version 2.
- Sleeve pattern: Follow chart. For Version 1, change contrast colors with every symbol change in this order: gold, rust, green. For Version 2, change contrast colors in this order: black, gold, green.

DIRECTIONS

Back

With smaller needles and MC, CO 108 (118, 122, 130) sts. Work 9 rows in St st. K 1 row on WS. Work 9 rows in border patt. Switch to larger needles and MC, work in St st, inc 1 st at each edge every 24 (26, 18, 24) rows 3 (2, 5, 2) times, then every 0 (28, 0, 26) rows 0 (1, 0, 2) times. Work until piece measures 11" (12", 12", 14") from CO edge. **Shape armhole:** BO 3 sts at the beg of the next 2 rows, then BO 2 sts at the beg of the next 4 rows. Dec 1 st at each edge as follows: 1 st every 26 (26, 0, 20) rows 2 (1, 0, 3) times, then every 0 (28, 0, 0) rows 0 (1, 0, 0) time. Work until armhole measures 7 1/2" (8", 8", 8"). **Shape neck:** work across 29 (34, 40, 40) sts, join second ball of yarn and BO next 38 sts, finish row. Working both sides at once with separate balls of yarn, BO 2 sts at each neck edge EOR twice. Work until each side measures 19½" (21", 21", 23") from CO edge, then place each group of 25 (30, 36, 36) shoulder sts on a stitch holder.

Front

Make 1 and 1 reversed. CO 48 (54, 55, 60) sts. Work as for back, except at center front border edge, inc 1 st on hem EOR 5 times, then after turning row, dec 1 st EOR 5 times. When armhole measures 6½" (7", 7", 7"), **shape neck:** for sizes **Extra Small** and **Medium,** at front edge, BO on EOR 6 sts once, 3 sts once, 2 sts twice, dec 1 st EOR 4 times; for sizes **Small** and **Large,** BO on EOR 6 sts once, 3 sts twice, 1 st once, 2 sts once, dec 1 st EOR 3 times. When armhole is the same length as back, place 25 (30, 36, 36) shoulder sts on a stitch holder.

Front Bands

With RS facing, smaller needles, and MC, pick up 3 sts for every 4 rows. Work 9 rows in border patt, and *at the same time,* inc 1 st at each edge EOR 5 times. Knit 1 row on WS, work 9 rows in St st, and *at the same time,* dec 1 st at each edge EOR 5 times. BO.

Neckband

Join shoulders using 3-needle BO. Pick up 96 sts around neck. Work to match front bands.

Sleeves

With CC, crochet a chain of 126 (132, 132, 132) loops. With larger needles and MC, pick up 1 st in each loop. Work in sleeve patt until piece measures 17 ¾" (18¼", 18¼", 18¾"). **Shape cap:** at each edge, BO 3 sts at beg of next 2 rows, then BO 2 sts at beg of next 4 rows. BO remaining 112 (118, 118, 118) sts.

Cuffs

Unravel crochet chain, placing sts on smaller needles. With MC, evenly dec 60 (62, 62, 62) sts; 66 (70, 70, 70) sts remain. Work to match front band (do not miter).

Finishing

Set in sleeves. Sew side and sleeve seams. Sew all borders together, keeping corners mitered as knitted. Hem borders. Steam lightly through pressing cloth.

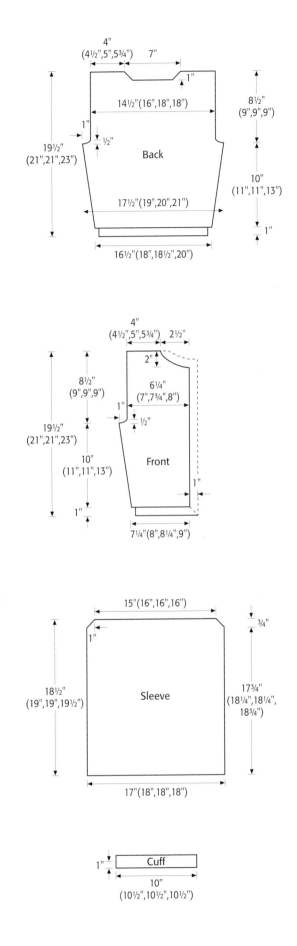

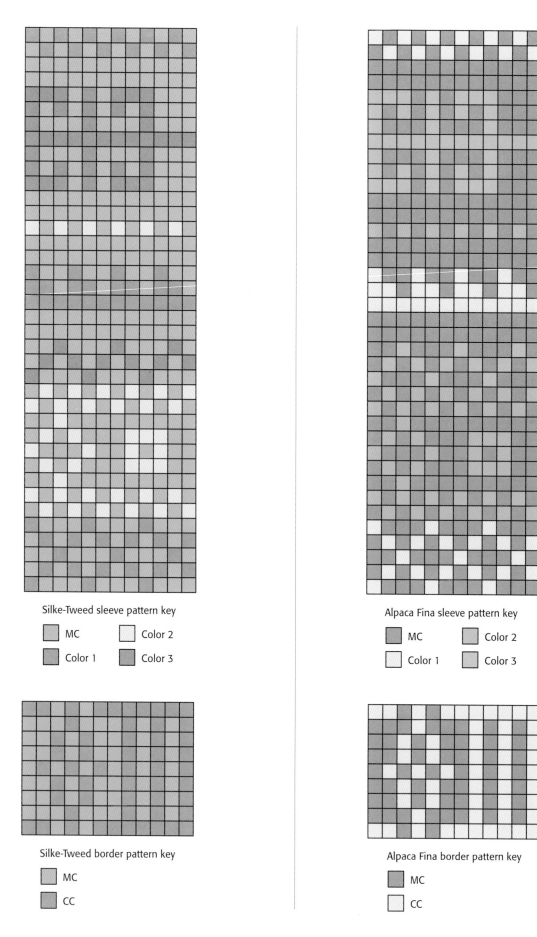

Silke-Tweed sleeve pattern key

▨ MC ▫ Color 2

▨ Color 1 ▨ Color 3

Alpaca Fina sleeve pattern key

▨ MC ▨ Color 2

▫ Color 1 ▨ Color 3

Silke-Tweed border pattern key

▨ MC

▨ CC

Alpaca Fina border pattern key

▨ MC

▫ CC

Shimmer Scarf

SKILL LEVEL
Beginner

✍

SIZE
One size

✍

FINISHED MEASUREMENTS
Approximately 13" x 60"

SHIMMER SCARF— *Tynn Chenille Pelsprint, Muskat, and Cotton Viscose*

YARN CHOICES

WELL, THIS PROJECT was interesting. What a difference a yarn can make! Look at the three versions of the Shimmer Scarf. Pelsprint is fun and funky. Muskat and Cotton Viscose are more sophisticated, even formal. I pictured the white Muskat version of the scarf and matching Petal Purse (page 00) for the bride, and the taupe Cotton Viscose version for the wedding guest. Remember the previous scarf explanation? A scarf is a scarf is a scarf. Make it as wide and long as you care to.

MATERIALS

All Versions

- 3 skeins of Garnstudio Tynn Chenille Pelsprint (41% cotton/42% viscose/17% acrylic, 50g/130yds)
  OR 3 skeins of Garnstudio Cotton Viscose (54% Egyptian cotton/46% viscose, 50g/120yds)
  OR 3 skeins of Garnstudio Muskat (100% Egyptian mercerized cotton, 50g/109yds)
- One pair of size 11 US (8.0mm) needles or size to obtain correct gauge

GAUGE

3 sts = 1" in Mock Turkish stitch
Take time to check gauge.

PATTERN STITCH

Mock Turkish Stitch

K 1, *YO, K2tog; rep from *, end K 1.
Rep this row.

DIRECTIONS

CO 40 sts. Knit 1 row. Work in pattern stitch until desired length. Knit 1 row. BO in patt.

LINEN STITCH VEST—*Paris and Cotton Frisé*

Linen Stitch Vest

SKILL LEVEL
Beginner

❧

SIZES
Extra Small (Small, Medium, Large)

❧

FINISHED MEASUREMENTS
Chest: 34" (38", 42", 46")
Length: 19" (21", 23", 23")

LINEN STITCH VEST—*Ull-Tweed*

Yarn Choices

I F T W O V E S T S could ever look more different from each other, here they are! The Ull-Tweed version is very classic New England: warm, woolly, and traditional. The Paris/Cotton Frisé version reminds me of the Florida coast and sailing. What a difference fibers and colors make! You just never know what you can achieve until you start swatching. I tried quite a few different yarns and color combinations before finding these. Ull-Tweed has 50g/120 yds, and the average yardage of Paris (50g/82 yds) and Cotton Frisé (50g/158 yds) is 120 yds (82 + 158 = 240; 240 divided by 2 = 120). So, I figured I would give it a whirl—and it worked. Also, button choices make quite a statement here. I chose elk antler for the Ull-Tweed vest, and mother-of-pearl for the Paris/Cotton Frisé vest. The lesson here? Never skimp on the finishing details!

Materials

Version 1

- 3 (4, 4, 5) skeins of Garnstudio Karisma Ull-Tweed (100% wool, 50g/120yds) in #06-charcoal grey and 2 (3, 3, 3) skeins each in #04-russet and #01-natural
- One pair each of size 6 US (4.0mm) and size 8 US (5.0mm) needles, or *size to obtain correct gauge*

Version 2

- 5 (6, 7, 7) skeins of Garnstudio Paris (100% cotton, 50g/82yds) in #28-navy blue and 2 (3, 3, 3) skeins of Garnstudio Cotton Frisé (85% cotton/15% nylon, 50g/158yds) in #01-white
- One pair each of size 5 US (3.75mm) and size 8 US (5mm) needles, or *size to obtain correct gauge*

Both Versions

- Crochet hook, size D
- Stitch holders
- Four ½"-diameter buttons

Gauge

5.5 sts and 8.5 rows = 1" in Linen Stitch patt on larger needles

Take time to check gauge.

Pattern Stitch

Linen Stitch

Row 1 (RS): *K1, yf, sl 1 pw, yb; rep from *, end K2.
Row 2: *P1, yb, sl 1 pw, yf; rep from *, end P2.
Rep rows 1 and 2.

Notes

- For Version 1, alternate 2 rows of each color in the following sequence: *grey (MC), natural, grey, russet. Rep from *.
- For Version 2, alternate 2 rows of each yarn throughout. Paris is the MC.

Directions

Back

With smaller needles and MC, CO 96 (106, 118, 128) sts. Work 2 rows of patt. Switch to larger needles, join next color, and work in patt. Work until piece measures 11" (13", 14½", 14") from beg. **Shape armhole:** BO 3 sts at beg of each armhole edge 4 times, BO 2 sts 4 times, then dec 1 st at each end EOR 3 times until you have 70 (80, 92, 102) sts remaining. **Cont dec for sizes Small (Medium, Large):** dec 1 st at each end every 4 (2, 2) rows 5 (11, 12) times until you have 70 (70, 78) sts. Work until piece measures 18½" (20½", 22½", 22½") from CO edge. Work 20 (20, 20, 22) sts, join second ball of yarn and BO center 30 (30, 30, 34) sts, finish row. Working both sides at once with separate balls of yarn, BO 2 sts at each neck edge EOR twice. Each side should measure 19" (21", 23", 23") from CO edge. Place each group of 16 (16, 16, 18) shoulder sts on a stitch holder.

Fronts

Make 1 and 1 reversed. With smaller needles and MC, CO 48 (54, 60, 64) sts. Work 2 rows in patt. Switch to larger needles, join next color, and cont in patt as for back. When piece measures 11" (13", 14½", 14") from CO edge, shape armhole as for back; *at the same time,* **shape neck:** at neck edge, dec 1 st EOR 7 (7, 5, 5) times, then dec 1 st every 4 rows 12 (13, 15, 16) times. Work until piece measures same as back. Place 16 (16, 16, 18) shoulder sts on a stitch holder.

Finishing

Join shoulders using 3-needle BO. With crochet hook and MC, crochet armhole edges as follows: join yarn end at seam, work a single crochet in every other st around, work 1 reverse crochet in each single crochet around, fasten off. For body of garment, join yarn at right front edge. Work single crochet as for armhole. Then work 1 row of reverse single crochet as for armhole, making 4 button loops on right front by chaining 5 sts, starting 2" from bottom edge and evenly spacing them up to V point. Cont around neck, left front, and back. Fasten off. Sew in remaining ends. Sew on buttons, aligning holes of button with inner edge of crochet trim.

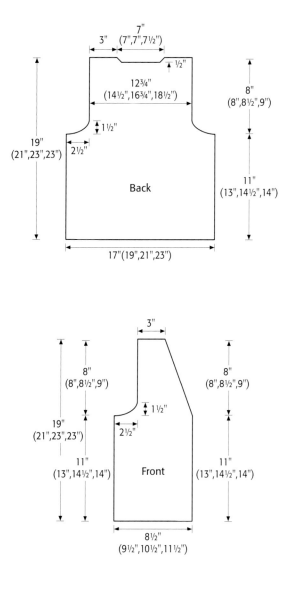

ZIPPERED JACKET—*Tynn Chenille Pelsprint and Pelliza*

Zippered Jacket

SKILL LEVEL
Beginner

∽

SIZES
Small (Medium, Large)

∽

FINISHED MEASUREMENTS
Chest: 40" (42", 44")
Length: 19" (19", 23")

ZIPPERED JACKET—*Karisma Classic and Vienna*

Yarn Choices

Wow, was I ever jazzed about this project! I am not one for animal prints, yet the Pelsprint gave me a taste of one without having to wear an animal-skin statement. I do enjoy my "furries," though—I have four cats and three dogs and just love the fluff—so I chose Pelliza to give that faux-fur look.

Version 2 had me stumped. Why would I want to do something conservative to contrast the animal statement I created? Well, the wool (Karisma Classic or Superwash) and mohair (Vienna) combination made me think otherwise. This is something that can carry you from the office to the opera. But, if you want, you can substitute the Pelliza for the Vienna, and go right out to the jazziest clubs in town.

MATERIALS

Version 1

- 9 (10, 11) skeins of Garnstudio Tynn Chenille Pelsprint (41% cotton/42% viscose/17% acrylic, 50g/130yds), and 2 skeins of Garnstudio Pelliza (100% polyester, 50g/125yds)
- One pair each of size 3 US (3.25mm) and size 4 US (3.5mm) needles, or *size to obtain correct gauge*

Version 2

- 13 (14, 15) skeins of Garnstudio Karisma Classic or Superwash (100% wool, 50g/120yds), and 1 skein of Garnstudio Vienna (90% mohair/10% polyester, 50g/103yds)
- One pair each of size 5 US (3.75mm) and size 8 US (5.0mm) needles, or *size to obtain correct gauge*

Both Versions

- 16" (16", 20") Drops separating zipper (see "Resources" on page 00)
- Matching thread and sewing needle

GAUGE

4.25 sts and 8.75 rows = 1" in garter stitch in
   Pelsprint or Karisma Classic on larger needles
6.5 sts and 8 rows = 1" in reverse St st in Pelliza
   on larger needles
4 sts and 5.25 rows = 1" in reverse St st in Vienna
   on larger needles
Take time to check gauge.

PATTERN STITCHES

Garter Stitch

Every row: Knit.

Reverse Stockinette Stitch

Row 1: Purl.
Row 2: Knit.
Rep rows 1 and 2. (The purl side is the right side.)

DIRECTIONS

Back

With smaller needles CO 88 (92, 96) sts. First row is RSR. Keep 1 st at each edge in St st as selvage. Knit 4 rows on smaller needles. Switch to larger needles. Work until piece measures 9" (9", 13") from CO edge. **Shape armhole:** at each armhole edge, dec 1 st EOR 4 times, then dec 1 st every 4th row 4 times. Cont until piece measures 9" from underarm. **Shape shoulders and neck:** at each shoulder edge, BO 5 (6, 6) sts EOR twice, then 5 (5, 6) sts twice; *at the same time,* when piece measures 18½" (18½", 22½"), BO 2 sts at each neck edge EOR twice. BO remaining 24 neck sts.

Front

Make 1 and 1 reversed. With smaller needles, CO 46 (48, 50) sts. First row is RSR. Keep 1 st at side seam in St st as selvage. Work as for back until piece measures 16" (16", 20") from CO edge. Shape armhole and shoulders as for back. **Shape neck:** at neck edge on EOR, BO 7 sts once, 2 sts 3 times, 1 st twice, work 2 rows, dec 1 st EOR twice, work 2 rows, dec 1 st once, work 4 rows.

Sleeves

With larger needles, CO 46 sts for all sizes. Work in garter st for 3". Inc 1 st at each edge every 8th row 14 (12, 10) times, then every 10th row 2 (4, 6) times. Work until piece measures 19" (19½", 20") from CO edge. **Shape sleeve cap:** *dec 1 st at each end of *every row* 4 times; skip the dec on 5th row; * rep from * to * 6 times total. Then dec 1 st at each end of *every row* 5 times. Work until 36 rows have been knitted. BO remaining 20 sts. Join shoulders using mattress stitch. Sew zipper in place.

Collar

With RS facing and size 4 needles for Version 1 or size 8 for Version 2, pick up 76 sts. Working in reverse St st, inc 1 st at each end of every 12th row 3 times until you have 82 sts. BO.

CONTRASTING COLLAR

Version 1

With Pelliza and larger needles, CO 118 sts. Working in reverse St st, inc 1 st at each end of every 7th row 5 times until you have 128 sts. BO.

Version 2

With Vienna and larger needles, CO 72 sts. Working in reverse St st, inc 1 st at each end of every 7th row 3 times until you have 78 sts. BO.

CONTRASTING CUFFS

Version 1

With Pelliza and larger needles, CO 72 sts. Work in reverse St st for 4". BO.

Version 2

With Vienna and larger needles, CO 44 sts. Work in reverse St st for 4". BO.

Finishing

Sew on cuffs: With RS of sleeve facing, measure ½" from CO edge and mark with straight pins for basting stitch. With knit side of cuff facing RS of sleeve, pin CO edge of cuff to marked line. Stitch in place. From stitching, measure 3½" up sleeve on WS and mark across. Fold cuff to WS and stitch in place along marked line. Sew full length of side seams. Sew cuff seam with mattress stitch. Fold up cuffs and tack in place if desired. **Attach collar:** With purl side of collar facing you, pin CO edge to inside of jacket collar just below where you picked up sts. Leave ¼" excess at each edge. Tuck tops of zipper in between 2 collars. Stitch CO edge of collar in place. Slightly stretch top of collar so it extends ¼" past top edge of jacket collar. Fold over and pin. Repeat for side edges of collar. Stitch side edges in place, then top edge.

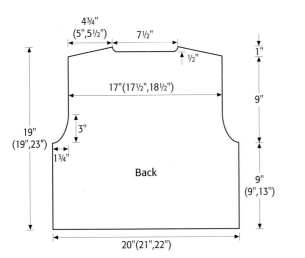

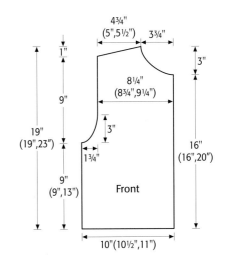

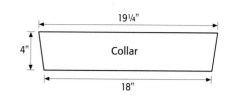

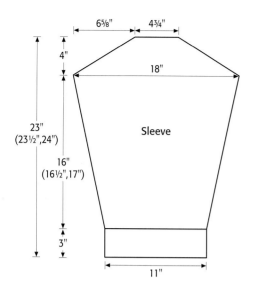

6⅝" 4¾"

4"

18"

Sleeve

23"
(23½", 24")

16"
(16½", 17")

3"

11"

19¼"

4"   Collar

18"

Petal Purse

SKILL LEVEL
Intermediate

❧

FINISHED MEASUREMENTS
6¾" x 6¾" with Muskat
6¼" x 6¼" with Cotton Viscose
or Safran

PETAL PURSE—*Cotton Viscose and Muskat*

YARN CHOICES

THE MUSKAT VERSION of the purse is slightly larger than the Cotton Viscose. But I decided, in keeping with my bridal theme, that the bride definitely needs to put more stuff in her bag than the average guest. So I can accept the differences here. The Cotton Viscose version is a smaller purse, yet extremely stylish and an asset to any wardrobe. You can also use Safran instead of the Cotton Viscose.

Materials

Both Versions

- 2 skeins of Garnstudio Muskat (100% mercerized Egyptian cotton, 50g/109yds)
  OR 2 skeins of Garnstudio Cotton Viscose (54% Egyptian cotton, 46% viscose, 50g/120yds)
  OR 2 skeins of Garnstudio Safran (100% Egyptian cotton, 50g/174yds)
- One pair of size 4 US (3.5mm) needles or *size to obtain correct gauge*
- Two size 4 US (3.5mm) double-pointed needles or *size to obtain correct gauge*
- Crochet hook, size E
- 7" x 15" piece of lining fabric for the Muskat version
  OR 6½" x 14" piece for the Cotton Viscose or Safran version
- Two ¼"-wide stays (available at fabric stores), 8" long for Muskat version, 7" long for Cotton Viscose or Safran version
- Matching sewing thread, sewing needle
- 3 snaps, size 2/0

Gauge

5 sts and 6.5 rows = 1" in reverse St st in Muskat

5.5 sts and 7.5 rows = 1" in reverse St st in Cotton Viscose or Safran

Take time to check gauge.

Pattern Stitch

CO 2 sts.

Row 1: K1, YO, K1.

Row 2: K1, P1, K1.

Row 3: (K1, YO) twice, K1.

Row 4: K1, P3, K1.

Row 5: (K1, YO) 4 times, K1.

Row 6: K1, P7, K1.

Row 7: K1, YO, P1, K2, YO, K1, YO, K2, P1, YO, K1.

Row 8: K1, P1, K1, P7, K1, P1, K1.

Row 9: K1, YO, P2, K3, YO, K1, YO, K3, P2, YO, K1.

Row 10: K1, P1, K2, P9, K2, P1, K1.

Row 11: K1, YO, P3, K4, YO, K1, YO, K4, P3, YO, K1.

Row 12: K1, P1, K3, P11, K3, P1, K1.

Row 13: K1, YO, P4, K5, YO, K1, YO, K5, P4, YO, K1.

Row 14: K1, P1, K4, P13, K4, P1, K1.

Row 15: K1, YO, P5, K6, YO, K1, YO, K6, P5, YO, K1.

Row 16: K1, P1, K5, P15, K5, P1, K1.

Row 17: K1, YO, P6, SSK, K11, K2tog, P6, YO, K1.

Row 18: K1, P1, K6, P13, K6, P1, K1.

Row 19: K1, YO, P7, SSK, K9, K2tog, P7, YO, K1.

Row 20: K1, P1, K7, P11, K7, P1, K1.

Row 21: K1, YO, P8, SSK, K7, K2tog, P8, YO, K1.

Row 22: K1, P1, K8, P9, K8, P1, K1.

Row 23: K1, YO, P9, SSK, K5, K2tog, P9, YO, K1.

Row 24: K1, P1, K9, P7, K9, P1, K1.

Row 25: K1, YO, P10, SSK, K3, K2tog, P10, YO, K1.

Row 26: K1, P1, K10, P5, K10, P1, K1.

Row 27: K1, YO, P11, SSK, K1, K2tog, P11, YO, K1.

Row 28: K1, P1, K11, P3, K11, P1, K1.

Row 29: K1, YO, P12, yb, sl 1, K2tog, psso, P12, YO, K1.

Row 30: K29.

Row 31: K1, YO, P27, YO, K1.
Row 32: K31.
Row 33: K1, YO, P29, YO, K1.
Row 34: K33.
BO as to purl, with RS facing.

DIRECTIONS

Purse

Make 8 triangles in patt stitch. Sew each set of 4 triangles together with WS facing you, using the knot-to-loop method shown below.

Lightly block with steam on WS. With WS of panels facing each other, mark 2½" down from top on both sides. Begin crocheting the two pieces together using reverse crochet (work a single crochet from left to right rather than from right to left) from one marked point to the other across the bottom. Cont crocheting along the single side of one panel, across the top to the opposite join. Rep crochet across top portion of other panel.

Purse Straps

With the two dpns, make two 44"-long I-cord straps as follows: CO 2 sts on 1 dpn. *Knit 1 row. Without turning work, slide the sts back to the beg of the needle. Pull the yarn tightly from the end of the row. Rep from * until piece measures 44". BO. Attach 2" of each end of I cord to inside edges of purse.

Lining

Fold the fabric in half lengthwise with right sides facing each other. Sew side seams, using a ⅜"-wide seam allowance, to within 3½" of top opening. Make casing as follows: Fold over ¾" to WS. Topstitch along top edge, then topstitch again ⅝" down from first stitching. Insert ¼" stays. To finish open side edges, fold to WS along ⅜" stitching line. Sew with edge stitch to base of opening.

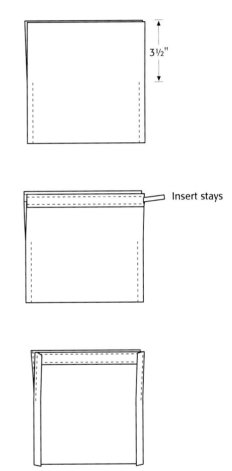

3½"

Insert stays

Finishing

Hand stitch lining into purse, aligning fabric to inside edges of crochet trim. Sew snaps in place, 1 in the center and 1 at each edge of purse.

Resources

DESIGNS BY CYNTHIA WISE
www.cynthiawise.com
cynthiawise@cynthiawise.com
122 Scoville Hill Road
Harwinton, CT 06791
phone/fax: 860-485-9489
Retail sales of all items contained in this book,
including yarns, buttons, zippers, and kits

AURORA YARNS
Frederikka Payne
aurorayarns@pacbell.net
PO Box 3068
2385 Carlos Street
Moss Beach, CA 94038
Wholesale distributor of Garnstudio Yarns
and pattern leaflets of Designs by Cynthia Wise

SCHAEFER YARN COMPANY
3514 Kelly's Corners Road
Interlaken, NY 14847
phone: 607-532-9452
Wholesale distributor of original hand-painted
yarns

LACIS
www.lacis.com
3163 Adeline Street
Berkeley, CA 94703
phone: 510-843-7178
Purse stays for Petal Purse

Bibliography

Butterick Company, Inc. *Vogue Knitting*. New York: Pantheon Books, 1989.

Stanley, Montse. *Reader's Digest Knitter's Handbook*. Pleasantville, N.Y.: The Reader's Digest Association, Inc., 1993.

Walker, Barbara G. *A Treasury of Knitting Patterns*. New York: Charles Scribner's Sons, 1968.

———. *A Second Treasury of Knitting Patterns*. New York: Charles Scribner's Sons, 1970.

Martingale & Company
Toll-free: 1-800-426-3126

International: 1-425-483-3313
24-Hour Fax: 1-425-486-7596

PO Box 118, Bothell, WA 98041-0118 USA

Web site: www.patchwork.com
E-mail: info@martingale-pub.com

Books from

These books are available through your local quilt, fabric, craft-supply, or art-supply store. For more information, contact us for a free full-color catalog. You can also find our full catalog of books online at www.patchwork.com.

Appliqué

Appliqué for Baby
Appliqué in Bloom
Baltimore Bouquets
Basic Quiltmaking Techniques for Hand Appliqué
Basic Quiltmaking Techniques for Machine Appliqué
Coxcomb Quilt
The Easy Art of Appliqué
Folk Art Animals
Fun with Sunbonnet Sue
Garden Appliqué
The Nursery Rhyme Quilt
Red and Green: An Appliqué Tradition
Rose Sampler Supreme
Stars in the Garden
Sunbonnet Sue All Through the Year

Beginning Quiltmaking

Basic Quiltmaking Techniques for Borders & Bindings
Basic Quiltmaking Techniques for Curved Piecing
Basic Quiltmaking Techniques for Divided Circles
Basic Quiltmaking Techniques for Eight-Pointed Stars
Basic Quiltmaking Techniques for Hand Appliqué
Basic Quiltmaking Techniques for Machine Appliqué
Basic Quiltmaking Techniques for Strip Piecing
The Quilter's Handbook
Your First Quilt Book (or it should be!)

Crafts

15 Beads
Fabric Mosaics
Folded Fabric Fun
Making Memories

Cross-Stitch & Embroidery

Hand-Stitched Samplers from I Done My Best
Kitties to Stitch and Quilt: 15 Redwork Designs
Miniature Baltimore Album Quilts
A Silk-Ribbon Album

Designing Quilts

Color: The Quilter's Guide
Design Essentials: The Quilter's Guide
Design Your Own Quilts
Designing Quilts: The Value of Value
The Nature of Design
QuiltSkills
Sensational Settings
Surprising Designs from Traditional Quilt Blocks
Whimsies & Whynots

Holiday

Christmas Ribbonry
Easy Seasonal Wall Quilts
Favorite Christmas Quilts from That Patchwork Place
Holiday Happenings
Quilted for Christmas
Quilted for Christmas, Book IV
Special-Occasion Table Runners
Welcome to the North Pole

Home Decorating

The Home Decorator's Stamping Book
Make Room for Quilts
Special-Occasion Table Runners
Stitch & Stencil
Welcome Home: Debbie Mumm
Welcome Home: Kaffe Fassett

Knitting

Simply Beautiful Sweaters
Two Sticks and a String

Paper Arts

The Art of Handmade Paper and Collage
Grow Your Own Paper
Stamp with Style

Paper Piecing

Classic Quilts with Precise Foundation Piecing
Easy Machine Paper Piecing
Easy Mix & Match Machine Paper Piecing
Easy Paper-Pieced Keepsake Quilts
Easy Paper-Pieced Miniatures
Easy Reversible Vests
Go Wild with Quilts
Go Wild with Quilts—Again!
It's Raining Cats & Dogs
Mariner's Medallion
Needles and Notions
Paper-Pieced Curves
Paper Piecing the Seasons
A Quilter's Ark
Sewing on the Line
Show Me How to Paper Piece

Quilting & Finishing Techniques

The Border Workbook
Borders by Design
A Fine Finish
Happy Endings
Interlacing Borders
Lap Quilting Lives!
Loving Stitches
Machine Quilting Made Easy
Quilt It!
Quilting Design Sourcebook
Quilting Makes the Quilt
The Ultimate Book of Quilt Labels

Ribbonry

Christmas Ribbonry
A Passion for Ribbonry
Wedding Ribbonry

Rotary Cutting & Speed Piecing

101 Fabulous Rotary-Cut Quilts
365 Quilt Blocks a Year Perpetual Calendar
All-Star Sampler
Around the Block with Judy Hopkins
Basic Quiltmaking Techniques for Strip Piecing
Beyond Log Cabin
Block by Block
Easy Stash Quilts
Fat Quarter Quilts
The Joy of Quilting
A New Twist on Triangles
A Perfect Match
Quilters on the Go
ScrapMania
Shortcuts
Simply Scrappy Quilts
Spectacular Scraps
Square Dance
Stripples Strikes Again!
Strips That Sizzle
Surprising Designs from Traditional Quilt Blocks

Traditional Quilts with Painless Borders
Time-Crunch Quilts
Two-Color Quilts

Small & Miniature Quilts

Bunnies by the Bay Meets Little Quilts
Celebrate! With Little Quilts
Easy Paper-Pieced Miniatures
Fun with Miniature Log Cabin Blocks
Little Quilts all Through the House
Living with Little Quilts
Miniature Baltimore Album Quilts
A Silk-Ribbon Album
Small Quilts Made Easy
Small Wonders

Surface Design

Complex Cloth
Creative Marbling on Fabric
Dyes & Paints
Fantasy Fabrics
Hand-Dyed Fabric Made Easy
Jazz It Up
Machine Quilting with Decorative Threads
New Directions in Chenille
Thread Magic
Threadplay with Libby Lehman

Topics in Quiltmaking

Bargello Quilts
The Cat's Meow
Even More Quilts for Baby
Everyday Angels in Extraordinary Quilts
Fabric Collage Quilts
Fast-and-Fun Stenciled Quilts
Folk Art Quilts
It's Raining Cats & Dogs
Kitties to Stitch and Quilt: 15 Redwork Designs
Life in the Country with Country Threads
Machine-Stitched Cathedral Windows
More Quilts for Baby
A New Slant on Bargello Quilts
Patchwork Pantry
Pink Ribbon Quilts
Quilted Landscapes
The Quilted Nursery
Quilting Your Memories
Quilts for Baby
Quilts from Aunt Amy
Whimsies & Whynots

Watercolor Quilts

More Strip-Pieced Watercolor Magic
Quick Watercolor Quilts
Strip-Pieced Watercolor Magic
Watercolor Impressions
Watercolor Quilts

Wearables

Easy Reversible Vests
Just Like Mommy
New Directions in Chenille
Quick-Sew Fleece
Variations in Chenille

1/00